OPPOSING VIEWPOINTS® SERIES

The Presidential Election Process

Other Books of Related Interest:

At Issue Series

Are American Elections Fair?

"Congress shall make no law ... abridging the freedom of speech, or of the press."

First Amendment to the U.S. Constitution

The basic foundation of our democracy is the First Amendment guarantee of freedom of expression. The Opposing Viewpoints Series is dedicated to the concept of this basic freedom and the idea that it is more important to practice it than to enshrine it.

OPPOSING VIEWPOINTS® SERIES

The Presidential Election Process

Tom Lansford, Book Editor

GREENHAVEN PRESS
An imprint of Thomson Gale, a part of The Thomson Corporation

THOMSON
GALE

Detroit • New York • San Francisco • New Haven, Conn. • Waterville, Maine • London

THOMSON
GALE

Christine Nasso, *Publisher*
Elizabeth Des Chenes, *Managing Editor*

For more information, contact:
Greenhaven Press
27500 Drake Rd.
Farmington Hills, MI 48331-3535
Or you can visit our Internet site at http://www.gale.com

Articles in Greenhaven Press anthologies are often edited for length to meet page requirements. In addition, original titles of these works are changed to clearly present the main thesis and to explicitly indicate the author's opinion. Every effort is made to ensure that Greenhaven Press accurately reflects the original intent of the authors. Every effort has been made to trace the owners of copyrighted material.

Cover photograph reproduced by permission of photos.com.

LIBRARY OF CONGRESS CATALOGING-IN-PUBLICATION DATA

The presidential election process / Tom Lansford, book editor.
p. cm. -- (Opposing viewpoints)
Includes bibliographical references and index.
ISBN-13: 978-0-7377-3892-6 (hardcover)
ISBN-13: 978-0-7377-3893-3 (pbk.)
1. Presidents--United States--Nomination. 2. Presidents--United States--Election.
3. Political campaigns--United States. I. Lansford, Tom.
JK521.P69 2008
324.60973--dc22

2007035066

ISBN-10: 0-7377-3892-8 (hardcover)
ISBN-10: 0-7377-3893-6 (pbk.)

Printed in the United States of America
10 9 8 7 6 5 4 3 2 1

Contents

Why Consider Opposing Viewpoints?

> *"The only way in which a human being can make some approach to knowing the whole of a subject is by hearing what can be said about it by persons of every variety of opinion and studying all modes in which it can be looked at by every character of mind. No wise man ever acquired his wisdom in any mode but this."*
>
> *John Stuart Mill*

In our media-intensive culture it is not difficult to find differing opinions. Thousands of newspapers and magazines and dozens of radio and television talk shows resound with differing points of view. The difficulty lies in deciding which opinion to agree with and which "experts" seem the most credible. The more inundated we become with differing opinions and claims, the more essential it is to hone critical reading and thinking skills to evaluate these ideas. Opposing Viewpoints books address this problem directly by presenting stimulating debates that can be used to enhance and teach these skills. The varied opinions contained in each book examine many different aspects of a single issue. While examining these conveniently edited opposing views, readers can develop critical thinking skills such as the ability to compare and contrast authors' credibility, facts, argumentation styles, use of persuasive techniques, and other stylistic tools. In short, the Opposing Viewpoints series is an ideal way to attain the higher-level thinking and reading skills so essential in a culture of diverse and contradictory opinions.

In addition to providing a tool for critical thinking, Opposing Viewpoints books challenge readers to question their own strongly held opinions and assumptions. Most people form their opinions on the basis of upbringing, peer pressure, and personal, cultural, or professional bias. By reading carefully balanced opposing views, readers must directly confront new ideas as well as the opinions of those with whom they disagree. This is not to simplistically argue that everyone who reads opposing views will—or should—change his or her opinion. Instead, the series enhances readers' understanding of their own views by encouraging confrontation with opposing ideas. Careful examination of others' views can lead to the readers' understanding of the logical inconsistencies in their own opinions, perspective on why they hold an opinion, and the consideration of the possibility that their opinion requires further evaluation.

Evaluating Other Opinions

To ensure that this type of examination occurs, Opposing Viewpoints books present all types of opinions. Prominent spokespeople on different sides of each issue as well as well-known professionals from many disciplines challenge the reader. An additional goal of the series is to provide a forum for other, less-known, or even unpopular viewpoints. The opinion of an ordinary person who has had to make the decision to cut off life support from a terminally ill relative, for example, may be just as valuable and provide just as much insight as a medical ethicist's professional opinion. The editors have two additional purposes in including these less-known views. One, the editors encourage readers to respect others' opinions—even when not enhanced by professional credibility. It is only by reading or listening to and objectively evaluating others' ideas that one can determine whether they are worthy of consideration. Two, the inclusion of such viewpoints encourages the important critical thinking skill of objectively evaluating an author's credentials and bias. This evaluation will illuminate an author's reasons for taking a particular stance on an issue and will aid in readers' evaluation of the author's ideas.

It is our hope that these books will give readers a deeper understanding of the issues debated and an appreciation of the complexity of even seemingly simple issues when good and honest people disagree. This awareness is particularly important in a democratic society such as ours in which people enter into public debate to determine the common good. Those with whom one disagrees should not be regarded as enemies but rather as people whose views deserve careful examination and may shed light on one's own.

Thomas Jefferson once said that "difference of opinion leads to inquiry, and inquiry to truth." Jefferson, a broadly educated man, argued that "if a nation expects to be ignorant and free ... it expects what never was and never will be." As individuals and as a nation, it is imperative that we consider the opinions of others and examine them with skill and discernment. The Opposing Viewpoints series is intended to help readers achieve this goal.

David L. Bender and Bruno Leone,
Founders

Introduction

> *"The American people have now spoken, but it's going to take a little while to determine what they've said."*
>
> —*Bill Clinton*

On November 7, 2000, America went to the polls to elect a new president. There were two main candidates, Texas governor George W. Bush of the Republican Party and vice president Al Gore of the Democratic Party. The morning after the election, many people were surprised to learn that a victor still had not been determined in the balloting. Gore received the majority of the popular vote (the total number of individual votes) with just over 51 million votes, while Bush secured 50.5 million, but Bush had 271 electoral votes to Gore's 266. Meanwhile, Green Party candidate Ralph Nader received 2.8 million popular votes, but none in the electoral college. It would be more than a month before Bush was declared the official winner.

The election highlighted many of the flaws and problems with the presidential election system, as well as revealing its strengths and benefits. The controversies over the election results were the culmination of a number of other issues that emerged during the campaign. Incumbent president Bill Clinton was unable to seek a third term because of constitutional restrictions, therefore the race for the presidency was initially wide open. Gore had been vice president for eight years and was popular within the Democratic Party; consequently, few other Democrats wanted to compete with him for the nomination. He was challenged by Senator Bill Bradley of New Jersey and a number of minor candidates. Some Democrats complained about the lack of choices.

The party chose its candidate through a series of state elections. Some states used primaries, others caucuses. In the primaries, individual voters cast ballots for their choice, while in the caucuses, representatives of the party met and voted for their preferred candidate. The first caucus was held in Iowa, and Gore received 63 percent of the vote to Bradley's 37 percent. The first primary was conducted in New Hampshire, where Gore secured 49.7 percent to Bradley's 45.6 percent. Gore went on to build a commanding lead over Bradley, who dropped out of the race and endorsed the vice president. Bradley declared that "our party is strongest when we're unified, when we speak with one voice, when we work to guarantee a Democratic Congress and a Democratic president."

Bush faced a number of other Republicans in the nomination contest, including Arizona senator John McCain, businessman Steve Forbes, former government official Alan Keyes, and former vice president Dan Quayle, among others. Bush won the Iowa caucus with 41 percent to Forbes's 30 percent and Keyes's 14 percent, but McCain defeated the Texas governor 48 percent to 30 percent in the New Hampshire primary. Like Gore, however, Bush quickly built a large lead over the others who dropped out of the race. Many people criticized both the Iowa and New Hampshire contests and charged that these two small states had an undue influence on the selection process for both parties since the populations of the two states were not representative of the rest of the country. The result was two candidates who were not very different on most major issues. The similarities between Bush and Gore prompted Nader to enter the race, even though most observers did not believe he could win without the support of one of the two major parties.

Gore and Bush were confirmed as their party's presidential candidates at national conventions during the summer of 2000. Most of the two conventions was broadcast on television, and the events served as a means to highlight the prospective candidates and their political plans. By the time of the conventions, Bush had raised $91 million, while Gore had secured $49 million. The top losing candidates in fundraising were Forbes, with $48 million; McCain, $45 million; and Bradley, $42 million. Both Bush and Gore continued to raise record amounts of campaign contributions. By election day in November, Bush had garnered more than $191 million, while Gore had $131 million.

The conventions marked the start of the main presidential election campaign. Through a series of debates and ever more contentious campaign advertising, both Gore and Bush attempted to paint each other as an extremist and portray themselves as the candidate most in touch with the American people and best able to get things done. In their October 11, 2000, presidential debate, in his closing remarks, Gore declared, "This race is about values, it's about change, it's about giving choices to the American people." Bush stated, "I'm running to get some things done for America. There's too many issues left unresolved.... I would like to unite this country to get an agenda done that will speak to the hopes and aspirations of the future."

In the United States, the president is formally chosen by the electoral college. Voters in each state cast ballots for their chosen candidates, and whoever receives the most votes gets all of that state's electoral votes. The number of electoral votes in each state is determined by a state's population as represented by its congressional delegation. For instance, Virginia has two senators and eleven members of the House of Representatives and therefore has thirteen electoral votes. Montana has three electoral votes; California, fifty-five, Texas, thirty-four, and so forth.

On election day in 2000, Gore led Bush in the popular vote, but Bush had more electoral votes; however, in Florida only five hundred votes separated Bush, the state's winner, and Gore. The Democrats demanded a recount. As was permitted under Florida law, Gore chose which counties would have their votes recounted by hand. He picked four south Florida counties that were primarily Democratic. During the recount, county officials often had to try to guess the intention of the voter if the ballot had errors or problems. The recount was actually televised so that Americans could see the election officials holding ballots up to the light for markings or "hanging chads" (pieces of the ballot that normally were stamped through when a voter chose a candidate, but in some cases remained attached to the voter's card). Republicans and Democrats took various aspects of the recount to court as the process wore on. Finally, on December 12, the Supreme Court, in a five-to-four ruling, declared that Florida could certify its final count, which gave Bush the election (a later recount found that Bush had won the state by 537 votes). In response, Bush stated that "I was not elected to serve one party, but to serve one nation. The president of the United States is the president of every single American, of every race and every background. Whether you voted for me or not, I will do my best to serve your interests and I will work to earn your respect."

Although the delay caused the country anxiety and slowed the presidential process, it also demonstrated the resilience of the country's institutions. A candidate had won a majority of the popular vote, but lost the electoral vote, yet the machinery of government continued without revolution or insurrection. In response to the decision of the Supreme Court, Gore offered these sentiments: "Now the U.S. Supreme Court has spoken. Let there be no doubt, while I strongly disagree with the court's decision, I accept it. I accept the finality of this outcome which will be ratified next Monday in the Electoral College. And tonight, for the sake of our unity of the people and the strength of our democracy, I offer my concession." And with his concession, the process moved on, and Bush took the oath of office on January 20, 2001.

The presidential election process continues to be the subject of great debate and controversy among Americans. Many argue that elections like that of 2000 demonstrate the need for reform and revision to the system. Others contend that the 2000 election showcased the strength of the presidential election process. The selections in *Opposing Viewpoints: The Presidential Election Process* explore the issues surrounding how the nation chooses its leader. The authors examine issues that revolve around four themes described by the following chapter titles: Does the Nomination Process Produce the Best Candidates? Should Campaign Spending Be Limited? Do the Media Unfairly Influence Presidential Campaigns? Should the Electoral College Be Abolished or Reformed? These types of concerns may be contested for some time, but the very fact that debate will go on underscores the vibrancy of the U.S. political process. As Gore said in his 2000 concession speech, "The strength of American democracy is shown most clearly through the difficulties it can overcome."

OPPOSING VIEWPOINTS® SERIES

CHAPTER 1

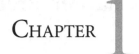

Does the Nomination Process Produce the Best Candidates?

Chapter Preface

Ideally the presidential nomination process provides a means for political parties, working with the American people, to choose the best presidential candidates. In order to become their party's choice for the presidency, candidates have to undergo extensive scrutiny by the media, raise large amounts of money, and win a majority of primaries and caucuses. The candidate is formally chosen at the party's national convention, which then serves as a springboard into the general campaign. It has become customary for the leading candidates from the major parties to engage in a series of public debates over the issues of the day, and since the 1950s these debates have been televised. This allows Americans to ascertain where the presidential hopefuls stand on major issues and to get a sense of their personalities. By election day, most Americans are very familiar with the candidates and able to make a rational choice for who should serve in the presidency.

Some Americans, however, believe that this system not only does not produce the optimum candidates, but that it actually prevents the best and brightest from winning their party's nomination. Many of the complaints about the system focus on the need for candidates to raise very large sums of money and therefore spend the majority of their time as fundraisers, rather than on developing new policies or crafting solutions to the nation's problems. In addition, the contemporary primary election system allows a handful of states to have an undue influence on the selection of the nominee. States such as New Hampshire and Iowa, which have the first round of primaries and caucuses, do not reflect the diversity of the United States, critics argue. Their populations tend to be largely white, wealthy, and rural. Also, because of the primary and caucus schedule, the party's nominee is usually decided long before the actual convention. As presidential historian

Michael Beschloss points out, in the past "conventions really did business, you had situations where the delegates were divided and you would have ballot after ballot before there was a final nominee." But in today's environment, the convention is often more of a coronation of a candidate rather than a forum where the candidate is actually chosen.

In the following chapter, journalists, political scientists, and other commentators explore the current process to select presidential candidates. They explore the primary and caucus systems, the party conventions, and other issues surrounding the nomination procedures. The debate in this chapter focuses on whether or not the contemporary selection process produces the best candidates.

VIEWPOINT 1

> *"The presidential nominating process is not perfect, but in recent decades it has enhanced participation ... and strengthened the tie between the average partisan and the candidates."*

The Nomination Process Produces Strong Presidential Candidates

Stephen J. Wayne

Historically, the political parties usually did not choose a presidential candidate until their nomination convention. In the viewpoint that follows, Stephen J. Wayne argues that reforms in the selection process have allowed strong candidates to gain an advantage and secure the nomination early in the process. While this has reduced the drama of the conventions, it has tended to produce better candidates with greater appeal to the party's base. Wayne is a professor of government at Georgetown University and the author of The Road to the White House 2004.

As you read, consider the following questions:

1. How did the advent of television affect the presidential candidates, according to Wayne?

Stephen J. Wayne, "Presidential Nominations and American Democracy," *Elections 2004*, United States Department of State, September 2003. http://usinfo.state.gov.

2. Have reforms in the nomination process strengthened or weakened the power of state party organizations, in the author's opinion?
3. According to Wayne, what are the main purposes of modern nomination conventions?

The system for nominating candidates for the U.S. presidency looks complex, even chaotic, and it is. Ever since the 1970s when the Democratic and Republican parties began to reform the rules for selecting their presidential and vice presidential nominees, the system has been in a state of flux, with the most successful candidates being those who understand the complexities and can maneuver in and around them. But after all, that is what creative politicians do—learn the game of politics and play it hard and skillfully.

The History of Nominations

Unlike the electoral college system for *electing* the president, the procedures for nominating presidential candidates are not spelled out in the U.S. Constitution. There were no political parties in existence at the time that the Constitution was drafted and ratified in the late 1700s. Parties developed after the government began to function, and as a consequence of the policies pursued by America's first president, George Washington.

Beginning in 1796, members of the U.S. Congress who identified with one of the political parties of the time met informally to agree on their party's presidential and vice presidential nominees. Known as "King Caucus," this system for selecting party candidates continued for almost 30 years. It broke down in 1824, a victim of the decentralization of power within the political parties that accompanied the westward expansion of the United States.

National nominating conventions replaced King Caucus. In 1831, a small and minor party, the Anti-Masons, met in a saloon in the city of Baltimore, Maryland, to choose candidates and a platform (a declaration of the principles and policies adopted by a political party or candidate) on which they would run. The next year, the Democrats met in the same saloon to select their nominees. Since then, the major parties and most minor parties have held national nominating conventions, attended by state delegates, to choose their presidential and vice presidential candidates and to agree on their policy positions.

Throughout the 19th and into the 20th century, the nominating conventions were controlled by state party leaders who used their influence to handpick their state's delegates and make sure that they voted "correctly" at the convention. The dominance of these party leaders ultimately became an issue within the parties. Those who did not like having entrenched "bosses" dictating the nominees supported reforms that permitted partisans within the states to select convention delegates in "primary" elections—elections that were scheduled before the general election. By 1916, more than half the states held presidential primaries.

The movement to encourage more people who considered themselves partisans to participate in their party's presidential selection process was short-lived, however. Following the end of World War I, party leaders, who saw the primaries as a threat to their power, persuaded state legislatures to abolish them on the grounds that they were expensive and that relatively few people participated in them. Some potential candidates had also refused to enter the primaries because they already had the support of state party leaders and did not want to risk losing that support in a popular vote. Besides, in some states the presidential preference vote was only advisory; convention delegates were selected in another manner. By 1936, only a dozen states continued to hold presidential primaries.

The Modern System

But democratizing pressures reemerged after World War II, aided by developments in communications technology. The advent of television provided a medium through which people could now see and hear the political campaigns in their own living rooms. Candidates could use television exposure to demonstrate their charismatic popularity and potential electability. As candidates, Dwight Eisenhower, John Kennedy, and Richard Nixon all entered multiple state primaries, at considerable cost and effort, to prove to their party that a general, a Catholic, and a once-defeated presidential candidate could win a general election. And they were successful. Each of them subsequently received his party's nomination and was elected president.

In addition, the Vietnam War, which began in the mid-1960s and continued into the 1970s, engendered internal divisions within the Democratic Party, which, in turn, created pressures for further reform. The catalyst was the 1968 Democratic nominating process. An anti-war movement split the Democratic Party and produced violent demonstrations in the streets of Chicago, the city that hosted the party's convention that year. Despite the agitation that accompanied its meeting, the party selected Vice President Hubert Humphrey, who had decided not to enter any Democratic primaries and thereby become a target of the anti-war protests.

Democratic Reforms

In an attempt to unify a divided party, the Democratic convention, after it nominated Humphrey, agreed to appoint a committee to reexamine the party's presidential nomination process, with the twin goals of encouraging greater party participation in the selection of a Democratic nominee and more equitable representation of the party at its nominating convention. The reforms adopted by the party began a process by which both major parties have democratized the way they select their nominees.

The major reforms that the Democrats instituted have encouraged most of the states, which make the election laws for their residents, to hold primary elections. As currently constituted, a primary is an election among supporters of the same party to choose that party's nominees to run in the general election. Depending on the laws of the state, voters may cast ballots for a party's presidential candidates themselves, or indirectly for convention delegates who are "pledged" to those candidates.

The only other option that states may have under the current system is to hold a multistaged caucus/convention process in which partisans who live within a relatively small geographic area—a local precinct—get together and vote for delegates who are pledged to support specific candidates. These delegates, in turn, represent their precinct at a county convention, which chooses delegates to attend the state convention. And the delegates to the state convention select delegates to represent the state at the national convention. Although this system involves several months, the candidate preferences are essentially determined in the first round of voting.

The actual size of any state's delegation to the national nominating convention is calculated on the basis of a formula established by each party that includes such considerations as the state's population, its past support for the party's national candidates, and the number of elected officials and party leaders currently serving in public office. The allocation formula that the Democrats use results in national conventions that have about twice as many delegates as those of the Republicans.

Decline of State Parties

The U.S. Constitution gives the states the authority to make their own election laws subject to the rules and qualifications

The Locations of Modern Party Conventions, 1960–2008

	Republican Party	*Democratic Party*
2008	Minneapolis, Minnesota	Denver, Colorado
2004	New York, New York	Boston, Massachusetts
2000	Philadelphia, Pennsylvania	Los Angeles, California
1996	San Diego, California	Chicago, Illinois
1992	Houston, Texas	New York, New York
1988	New Orleans, Louisiana	Atlanta, Georgia
1984	Dallas, Texas	San Francisco, California
1980	Detroit, Michigan	New York, New York
1976	Kansas City, Missouri	New York, New York
1972	Miami Beach, Florida	Miami Beach, Florida
1968	Miami Beach, Florida	Chicago, Illinois
1964	San Francisco, California	Atlantic City, New Jersey
1960	Chicago, Illinois	Los Angeles, California

that Congress may establish. Although states are free to determine the dates on which their primary and caucus elections may be held, they also have an incentive to conduct their nomination contests in accordance with party rules, since the U.S. Supreme Court has determined that the parties have a right to describe and enforce their own rules for those attending the national conventions. Thus, states that permit selection of party convention delegates in a manner that does not conform to party rules may find their delegates challenged when they get to the national party conventions, or they may find the size of the delegation reduced by the party for violating its rules.

Today, more than 80 percent of the delegates who attend their party's national convention are chosen in primary elections that are open to all registered or self-identified Democrats or Republicans.

The Democratic Party has imposed a set of national rules on all its state affiliates, the Republican Party has not. The Democratic rules, in effect, require states to hold their presidential nomination contests between the first Tuesday of February and the second Tuesday in June in a presidential election year. The smaller states of Iowa and New Hampshire are given official exemptions to vote earlier because of their tradition of holding the first caucus and primary, respectively. The Democrats—in order to enhance the representation of minorities that may be concentrated in communities within the state—also require that 75 percent of a state's delegation be elected in districts that are no larger than a congressional district. Moreover, the number of delegates who are pledged to support specific candidates is determined in proportion to the vote they or their candidates receive. The Democrats also have other delegates—party leaders and elected officials—who are not under obligation to support particular candidates even though those candidates may have won primaries in their states. Finally, the Democrats require that state delegations be equally divided between men and women.

Party Differences

Despite the differences in party rules—the Republicans defer to their state affiliates and the Democrats do not—two important trends stand out:

- More and more states have moved their primaries and caucuses toward the beginning of the electoral process in order to exercise more influence over the selection of the nominees, encourage the candidates to address the needs and interests of the state, and get their campaigns to spend money in them. This is known as "front-loading."
- In a practice known as "regionalization," states have cooperated with one another to hold their primaries and caucuses on the same date to maximize the influence of a region.

Both of these trends have forced candidates to begin their campaigns earlier to gain a foothold in the states that hold the initial contests. Candidates also have had to depend increasingly on the mass media, particularly radio and television, and on the endorsements of state party leaders to help them reach voters in the multiple states that may be conducting their primaries on the same day.

The front-loading and the regionalization of the presidential primary nomination process has benefited nationally recognized candidates, such as incumbent presidents, the governors of major states, and U.S. senators and representatives who have access to money, media, and organizational support.

Modern Reforms

Consider the preliminaries leading up to the 2004 Democratic presidential nomination, for example. Eight Democratic candidates had raised approximately $25 million and had spent $7 million by March 31, 2003, more than 10 months before the first scheduled caucus or primary. Of these candidates, those who hold seats in the Congress raised the most, hired the best-known political consultants, and began to build the largest campaign organizations. The short time frame of the primary process works against those who need primaries and caucuses to be stepping-stones to the nomination, such as Jimmy Carter in 1976 and John McCain in 2000.

The continuing changes in the nomination process affect all the candidates. Even incumbent presidents cannot take their renomination for granted. In 1992, George H.W. Bush suffered some embarrassing defeats in the primaries at the hands of conservative talk show pundit and newspaper columnist Pat Buchanan. In contrast, Bill Clinton in 1996 raised large sums of money early on to discourage a political opponent within his own party from challenging him. Clinton used this money to pursue a strategy of mounting a media-oriented, electoral campaign that extended from the beginning of the caucuses and primaries through the national election.

Nominations

Reforms in the presidential nominating process have clearly enlarged the base of public participation. In 1968, before the recent changes in the process, only 12 million people voted in primaries, approximately 11 percent of the voting-age population. In 2000, approximately 35 million participated, about 15 percent of the electorate. In the run-up to the 2000 presidential election, more than 20 million voted in contests between George W. Bush and his Republican opponents, and about 15 million voted in the Democratic contests between Vice President Al Gore and his principal opponent, former Senator Bill Bradley.

In addition to increasing public participation, the modern nominating process has expanded the representation of the groups comprising each party's electoral coalition. Although demographic representation—in the sense of race and gender—has broadened among the parties' delegates to the nominating conventions, ideological representation has not. The reason for this is that those who have higher participation rates in the nomination process tend to be party activists who are more ideological than the average rank-and-file party identifiers. Thus, the delegates at Republican conventions tend to be more conservative and the Democratic delegates more liberal than their respective electorates.

As noted, the reforms have also weakened the power of state party leaders and provided incentives for those seeking their party's nomination to make broad-based public appeals. These appeals have strengthened the tie between the candidates and their core base supporters and have encouraged those who win office to redeem their campaign promises. George W. Bush, in his first year in office, directed his energies toward achieving his principal campaign policy goals of tax relief, educational reform, and greater military preparedness, policy initiatives oriented toward his conservative political base.

Although many of the nomination reforms have contributed to a democratization of the nomination process, anomalies still exist. Those who participate in the primary elections tend to be better educated, to have higher incomes, and to be older than the average Republican and Democratic voter. In addition, as always, those who contribute money to the candidates or for their causes tend to be in the higher socioeconomic brackets. Inevitably, they gain a more powerful voice in the election outcome as a result.

Finally, the public and contentious nomination process produces factions within the parties. The more competitive the quest for the nomination, the more likely that these divisions will develop to the point where they must be overcome quickly if a party is to mount a successful presidential campaign for its nominee.

Decline of the Conventions

Another consequence of the changes in the presidential nomination process has been the decreasing importance of the party's national nominating convention. Today, the presidential nominee is effectively determined by the voters relatively early in the nomination process. That nominee, in turn, usually indicates his choice for a vice presidential candidate before the convention meets. The winning candidate also controls the drafting of a party platform. Why, then, should the American people spend time in front of a television set watching the nominating conventions?

The fact of the matter is that many people do not do so. Convention viewership has declined in recent years, as have the number of hours that the major broadcast networks air the proceedings during prime viewing hours. Surveys conducted by research organizations during the summer of 2000, when both parties held their nominating conventions, found that about half the television audience did not tune in to either of them.

Continuing Convention Importance

Despite the decline in the viewing audience, the conventions still receive attention on news shows and in newspapers. The same surveys indicated that in 2000, public awareness increased during and after the conventions, as did knowledge of the candidates and their policies. Thus, the conventions did serve to inform the voters, shore up support and build enthusiasm among partisans for their party's nominees, and focus the attention of the country on the forthcoming general election.

The presidential nominating process is not perfect, but in recent decades it has enhanced participation, improved demographic representation, and strengthened the tie between the average partisan and the candidates. As constituted, he process gives advantage to candidates who are better known, can raise more money, have the most effective campaign organizations, and generate the most enthusiasm among the voters early in the presidential primary season.

VIEWPOINT 2

> *"[T]he nation is desperately in need of widespread change to and dramatic updating of the political system."*

The Current Nomination Process Should Be Replaced

Larry J. Sabato

In the following viewpoint Larry J. Sabato identifies a number of problems with the contemporary nomination process, including voter dissatisfaction and undue influence of certain states. He asserts that minor reforms are not enough to fix the system, and instead the nation needs to abandon the current manner of choosing presidents. Sabato is a noted political scientist at the University of Virginia and editor of Divided States of America: The Slash and Burn Politics of the 2004 Presidential Election.

As you read, consider the following questions:

1. Did the framers of the Constitution envision the modern political system, according to Sabato?
2. As stated by the author, what state traditionally has the first presidential primary?

Larry J. Sabato, "Politics: America's Missing Constitutional Link," *Virginia Quarterly Review*, vol. 82, no. 3, summer 2006, pp. 149–161. www.vqronline.org.

3. In the 2004 election cycle, what percentage of the population voted in the primaries and caucuses, according to Sabato?

The Constitution was written by the Founders when they had not yet realized the vital necessity of politics and parties in the process of our elections. Further, the enormous transformation of politics from the part-time avocation of public-spirited gentlemen to the multibillion-dollar enterprise of electoral institutions in a rich, diverse, continental Republic has not been matched by constitutional adaptation. The absence of modern politics in the Constitution—from the structure of presidential selection to the manner of congressional elections to some critical aspects of electioneering, such as redistricting and campaign finance—has caused no end of difficulties, which can only be corrected by the inclusion of thoughtful provisions in a new twenty-first-century Constitution. It is long past time to do so.

Critics of this constitutional approach may insist that the political inadequacies of our system are best handled through statutory means, the better to make adjustments as needed from time to time. And partly, this point of view has merit. The constitutional provisions on the political system should be kept only as specific as absolutely required to cure the ills discussed here. Congressional and state statutes—the regular lawmaking process in the various legislatures—can supplement mandates in the Constitution.

Chances for Reform

However, the chances for serious, widespread political reform at this late date are virtually nil without constitutional prodding. Yes, a state here or there may enact a useful reform plan for a piece of the puzzle. But the nation is desperately in need of widespread change to and dramatic updating of the political system. Entrenched interests would fight and stop most or all of the reforms outlined in this essay. The United States now has a massive superstructure of essentially untouchable procedures and traditions with powerful beneficiaries—incumbents, wealthy groups and individuals, even specific states (think Iowa and New Hampshire in the presidential selection process).

It will take a new revolution to modernize America's ossified politics. It will take a revolution generated by an engrossing national debate—the kind of debate that can only be engendered by the writing of a new Constitution. Enough with the Band-Aids! An end to feeble efforts at reform in one state or region! So much for the occasional initiative or referendum that usually fails due to campaign spending by special interests that would be damaged by change in the national interest. We the people need to confront all the problems at once, to seek a comprehensive solution that will be as permanent as a Constitution can promise.

Let's start by overhauling the insane methods we employ for picking a president.

Political Parties

Once avoided in their entirety by the Founders and the Constitution, political parties have become the sine qua non of American democracy. This was obvious by the time of Andrew Jackson, if not before. Even prior to his presidency, Woodrow Wilson declared parties to be utterly essential to the functioning of both elective branches—the institutions holding together the Government of the United States in the face of so many internal, dividing checks and balances:

> [G]overnment is not a machine, but a living thing.... No living thing can have its organs offset against each other as checks, and live.... The way in which the several branches of the federal government have been separately organized and given efficiency in the discharge of their own functions has only emphasized their separation and jealous indepen-

> dence.... It is for that reason that we have had such an extraordinary development [outside of the Constitution] of party authority in the United States and have developed outside the government itself so elaborate and effective an organization of parties. [The political parties] *are absolutely necessary to hold the things thus disconnected and dispersed together and give some coherence to the action of political forces.* [Emphasis added.]

Wilson also suggested the government was subject to Darwinian evolutionary forces, and he was correct again. Over many decades, the parties have evolved to meet the organizational needs of government. Along the way, though, the constitutionally ungoverned parties have also changed to serve their own needs better—and those selfish purposes have begun to override those of the citizenry's. Without any federal constitutional guidelines and strictures, parties have become *state-based*, even though they serve the highest of *national* purposes, such as the nomination of presidents. The fifty state political parties on each side (Democratic and Republican) squabble among themselves, initiating internecine battles about who can go first, and second, and third, in presidential selection every four years. In doing so, they promote and serve individual state interests over the national interest. The federal Constitution has been preeminent over the state constitutions since the days of Chief Justice John Marshall, but not so among the political parties, which live in a no-man's-land—a Wild, Wild West—in law and practice. Darwinian evolution is fine for the origin of species, but it is past time for the essential political institutions called *parties* to be governed by some sort of federal intelligent design. Only the Constitution can achieve this aim.

Presidential Primaries

If any ongoing disaster can prove the point, then surely it is the quadrennial orgy of the presidential primary process.

Imagine that a convention of clowns met to design an amusing, crazy-quilt schedule to nominate presidential candidates. The resulting system would probably look much as ours does today. The incoherent organization of primaries and caucuses, and the candidates' mad-dash attempts to move around the map, would be funny if the goal—electing the leader of the free world—weren't so serious.

In 1968 there were seventeen state presidential primaries, a manageable number spread out from March until June. The voters could focus on their task, and often there was enough time between primaries (a couple of weeks or so) for mid-course corrections in the selection of a party nominee. In 2004 there were forty primaries, not counting the ones in DC and Puerto Rico, and for "Americans abroad," stretching from January through June—a six-month period of intense politicking, preceded by at least a year of equally intense, headline-grabbing maneuvering by the candidates.

To make matters worse, in a phenomenon called *front-loading*, the states are mainly rushing to the front of this already-elongated calendar, in order to maximize their impact on the choice of the party nominees. While only one state had a primary or caucus in January or February of 1980, by 2000 that number was nine, and by 2004, nineteen. In the presidential system, the old axiom that "the first shall be last, and the last shall be first" doesn't apply. With only a couple of modern exceptions (1976 on the Republican side in the Gerald Ford-Ronald Reagan battle and 1984 in the Democratic struggle between Walter Mondale and Gary Hart), the presidential nominees have been known well in advance of the party conventions, and usually the first handful of primary and caucus contests determine the winners.

Few want to go back to the bad old days when party "bosses" chose presidential candidates in smoke-filled rooms. (Yes, the bosses did well by selecting nominees such as Franklin Roosevelt, but they also picked the disastrous Warren G.

Findings of the Commission on Federal Electoral Reform

Because the races for the presidential nominations in recent elections have generally concluded by March, most Americans have no say in the selection of presidential nominees, and intense media and public scrutiny of candidates is limited to about 10 weeks. Moreover, candidates must launch their presidential bids many months before the official campaign begins, so that they can raise the $25 to $50 million needed to compete.

The presidential primary schedule therefore is in need of a comprehensive overhaul. A new system should aim to expand participation in the process of choosing the party nominees for president and to give voters the chance to closely evaluate the presidential candidates over a three- to four-month period. Improvements in the process of selecting presidential nominees might also aim to provide opportunities for late entrants to the presidential race and to shift some emphasis from Iowa and New Hampshire to states that more fully reflect the diversity of America.

Commission on Federal Electoral Reform,
Building Confidence in U.S. Elections, *September 2005.*

Harding.) Primaries and caucuses are now fundamental to our conception of popular democracy in presidential selection. But there is such a thing as too much popular democracy, if it is hopelessly disorganized.

Every attempt to bring order out of chaos has failed, and there have been many attempts to do so. In 2000, Republicans tried to pass a plan to give states incentives to hold *later* primaries and caucuses in an attempt to slow front-loading, but the plan failed to pass. For 2008 the Democrats have been hoping to bring about some reasonable reordering of the early contests by designating a handful of representative states to go first, but the attempt to dilute the impact of Iowa and especially New Hampshire has been falling apart.

Iowa and New Hampshire

A good-sized piece of the problem can be labeled "Iowa and New Hampshire." These two states seem to assume that the Constitution guarantees that they should go first, but a close reading of the text finds no such clause. The New Hampshire primary has been around since 1920, and it has arguably been very influential since 1952, when it played a role in both the decision of President [Harry] Truman not to seek reelection and Dwight Eisenhower's successful quest for the GOP [Republican] nomination. New Hampshire reprised its 1952 king-killing act in 1968, when Minnesota senator Eugene McCarthy came within a few percentage points of President [Lyndon B.] Johnson in the Democratic primary, leading in part to LBJ's decision shortly thereafter not to seek another term. The Iowa caucus has only played a role since 1968, and its true national debut came in 1972, when George McGovern scored well there on his way to a surprise, ill-fated Democratic nomination. Just four years later, the Iowa caucus propelled a little-known former Georgia governor, Jimmy Carter, to the Democratic nomination and the presidency, assisted also by Carter's subsequent narrow victory in New Hampshire. (Remarkably, Carter succeeded grandly while capturing less than thirty percent of the vote in Iowa and New Hampshire.)

The presidential selection process is a bonanza for both the Hawkeye and Granite States. It is an industry that produces tens of millions of dollars in spending from the campaigns. Candidates and their staffs often practically move into these states, and they bring thousands of reporters with them over time. The television and radio stations, the hotels, and the restaurants of Iowa and New Hampshire make a killing off of the business generated by their claim to political supremacy.

Moreover, all the candidates—and thus the eventual president—learn about their problems and needs, and make lots of promises to fix this and spend that and support ethanol. The presidential selection process is a gravy train for Iowa and New Hampshire, and they know it. The citizens of the leadoff states take their job as presidential screeners seriously, but then what citizens given this important task would not? The presidential candidates fully understand the game they are playing, and the absurdity of it. For example, Michael Dukakis, the 1988 Democratic presidential nominee, had this to say about Iowa in 2001:

> I spent 85 campaign days in the state of Iowa alone. Now, Iowa is a great state ... and they did very well by Mike Dukakis. But, 85 full campaign days in one state ... really doesn't make a hell of a lot of sense, does it?

The truth is that Iowa and New Hampshire have a franchise they are determined to keep at all costs. New Hampshire even has a law that requires its secretary of state to do whatever is necessary to keep its primary first, and Secretary William Galvin has threatened, if needed, to move the New Hampshire primary back into *the calendar year before the presidential election* to fulfill his mandate. No doubt Iowa would do the same. And we think the process takes too long already?

Constitutional Reform

Without a constitutional answer, there is simply no remedy to a situation that deteriorates every four years. Try as they might, the political parties cannot orchestrate a fix. In the end, they can only punish a recalcitrant Iowa and New Hampshire in minor ways, perhaps by cutting the size of their convention delegations or giving the delegates bad hotels and poor seating at the party conclaves. And that assumes the national parties have the will to do anything. After all, Iowa and New Hampshire are in catbird seats since both are now swing states in the November 2008 presidential election, and their collective twelve electoral votes can easily be the difference between victory and defeat in this closely divided era.

In addition, Congress arguably has no effective power to intervene in a state-based, party-centered nominating process, and even if the courts held that it did, Congress would be highly unlikely to step into that briar patch. The senators and representatives from Iowa and New Hampshire would be willing to do anything to stop reform, quite possibly with assistance from colleagues who would see their own presidential ambitions at stake. A senator who becomes a hero in Iowa and New Hampshire for saving the caucus and primary would be halfway to a presidential nomination! And realizing this, most or all of the senators with presidential aspirations would jump to back the Iowa/New Hampshire status quo—and it's a rare senator who doesn't get up in the morning and see a president in the mirror.

No, the only possible, comprehensive answer is a constitutional one. In the twenty-first century we the people need to do what the Founders didn't even consider doing in their pre-party, pre-popular-democracy age. The guiding principle should be one that all citizens, in theory, can readily embrace: Every state and region ought to have essentially an equal chance, over time, to influence the outcome of the parties' presidential nominations, and thus the selection of presidents. Why should two small, heavily white, disproportionately rural states have a hammerlock on the making of the president? Together, Iowa and New Hampshire are a mere 1.4 percent of the US population, and about 40 percent of their residents are rural—double the national proportion. Their average population of African Americans *and* Hispanics/Latinos is 3.6 percent, while the nation as a whole is 24.6 percent minority. Even if one assumes, incorrectly, that the two states are somehow representative of their Northeast and Midwest regions, the South and West (containing 55 percent of the country's people) are left entirely out of the critical opening window of presidential selection.

Beyond the equal-influence-over-time rule, the presidential selection process also ought to enable the states to spread out the contests over several months, thereby reducing front-loading and the low voter turnout that comes with it. In most recent cycles, the nominations have been all but decided by the first few weeks of voting, leaving large majorities of voters and states effectively disenfranchised. In 2000, for example, both Vice President Al Gore and Governor George W. Bush had all but cinched his party's nomination *before thirty-three states, including many of the largest, had even voted.* Understandably, this fact led an alienated public to tune out the process before they could become engaged and learn about all the men and women who would be president. Also in 2000—the last time both parties had multicandidate, highly competitive fields running for the presidency—a mere 17.7 percent of the adult population turned out to vote *in all primaries and caucuses, in both parties and all states combined.* This is a miserable showing, and it also contributes to the control of the nominating machinery of both parties by those well over on the left (Democrats) and the right (Republicans). The majority of the public that is gathered around the ideological center has been the first to become discouraged and disconnected in the past few decades, furthering the polarization that bedevils American politics. The construction of a nominating process that is inclusive and rational may contribute a great deal to broadening the level of participation in the primaries and caucuses.

That nominating process ought also to be focused, and compressed into the four months leading up to the party conventions. Presidential politics now takes fully one-fourth of a president's four-year term, and with the acceleration of front-loading, it soon may consume even more of it. Not only is this bad for the presidency as an institution, it causes the electorate to tire of the never-ending political campaign. It should be possible to create a system that flows from the first primaries and caucuses in April directly into August party conventions, and then into the Labor Day kickoff for the autumn general election. Not only is this not rocket science, it doesn't even qualify as elementary mathematics. It is easy, if the will and the means are present. The electorate must supply the will, and the Constitution should outline the means.

VIEWPOINT 3

> *"Delegate selection for the conventions has become more democratic.... Party bosses no longer have the same influence that they used to."*

National Conventions Accomplish a Range of Goals for Parties

Jonathan Mott and Shad Satterthwaite

In the following viewpoint Jonathan Mott and Shad Satterthwaite explain the development of the modern political party convention. The two assert that the conventions were a way to democratize the nomination process by allowing average citizens the ability to vote on a potential presidential candidate rather than just having elites in the party decide. Jonathan Mott is director of the Center for Instructional Design at Brigham Young University, and Shad Satterthwaite is a lecturer at the University of Oklahoma.

As you read, consider the following questions:

1. Which political party held the first national convention, as reported by the authors?

Jonathan Mott and Shad Satterthwaite, "How Did Party Conventions Come About and What Purpose Do They Serve?" *ThisNation.com*, February 22, 2007. www.thisnation.com. Reproduced by permission.

2. Why was the 1968 Democratic Convention in Chicago called the most "tumultuous" in American history, according to Mott and Satterthwaite?
3. What are the three main functions of modern nominating conventions, in the author's opinion?

In the early nineteenth century, a party's presidential candidate was nominated by a congressional caucus. Members of Congress from the same party would meet and recommend a nominee. The Anti-Mason party held the first political convention in 1831. The Anti-Masons had little congressional representation, so they held a general meeting in Baltimore with 116 delegates from thirteen states. They chose a nominee and discussed issues that would be part of their campaign.

The First Democratic Convention

The following year the Democratic-Republicans (now known as the Democrats) held their first convention in Baltimore. The primary purpose of this convention was to show popular support for Andrew Jackson and to select Martin Van Buren as his running mate. The Democratic-Republicans, and later their Republican opponents continued to hold conventions to nominate a candidate for president and discuss issues that were central to the party.

Party leaders were the primary players at the conventions. Public participation was minimal. State party bosses controlled delegate selection. Throughout the nineteenth century, conventions were used to broker the various interests and unite the divisions within the party. A lot of deal making took place behind closed doors and rank-and-file party members had little say in the process. During the Progressive movement in the early 1900s, reform oriented politicians began making demands for change. They hoped to make the nomination process more democratic.

In 1912, former president Theodore Roosevelt challenged incumbent William Howard Taft. Roosevelt won nine prima-

The Rules of the Republican Party

At the 2004 Convention, the Republican Party adopted a set of rules designed to demonstrate its inclusiveness as characterized by its opening statement:

> Be it resolved, that the Republican Party is the party of the open door. Ours is the party of liberty, the party of equality of opportunity for all and favoritism for none.
>
> It is the intent and purpose of these rules to encourage and allow the broadest possible participation of all voters in Republican Party activities at all levels and to assure that the Republican Party is open and accessible to all Americans.

The Republican National Committee, August 30, 2004.

ries compared to Taft's one and had captured over 40 percent of the delegates. Despite this, Taft still won the nod of the party bosses and got the nomination. In opposition to the boss dominated politics at the convention more states began to adopt primaries. Primaries, however, were not considered to be an important part of the nomination process. State primaries were considered "beauty contests" used to demonstrate a candidate's popularity, but they were not necessarily key to getting a nomination.

Primaries

The comparative irrelevance of primaries changed dramatically after 1968. Senator Eugene McCarthy, running on an antiwar platform, challenged Lyndon Johnson in the New Hampshire primary. To the surprise of many, McCarthy received over 42 percent of the vote. Four days after McCarthy's strong showing, Robert Kennedy, another antiwar senator declared his candidacy. With opposition to the war mounting, Johnson bowed out of the election, clearing the way for his vice president, Hubert Humphrey to run. Hoping to get the nomination at the national convention. Humphrey intentionally prolonged his announcement and precluded a primary.

The 1968 Democratic National Convention was probably the most tumultuous political convention in the modern era. [civil rights leader] Martin Luther King Jr. and [presidential candidate] Robert Kennedy were both assassinated in the spring of that year. Convention delegates meeting in Chicago were sharply divided over the war in Vietnam. To make matters worse, thousands of protesters calling for an end to the war were marching in the streets of Chicago. Clashes between the protesters and police eventually erupted and were broadcast on national television.

Humphrey could not match the grassroots organization that McCarthy had, but he did have the support of most state party bosses. When it became clear that Humphrey would likely receive the nomination, many delegates felt cheated. They demanded and got promises to reform the convention process. The convention approved the establishment of a party committee to examine current rules and make recommendations designed to broaden participation. This committee became known as the McGovern-Fraser Commission.

McGovern-Fraser Commission

Chaired by Senator George McGovern and Congressman Donald Fraser, the commission recommended that registered Democratic voters should have "the maximum feasible opportunity to participate in the delegate selection process." The commission also recommended that women, minorities and young people should be represented based on the proportion of their population within each state. There were also other suggestions designed to make the nomination process more democratic.

In the wake of the McGovern-Fraser Commission's recommendations, the Republican National Committee established the Delegates and Organization Committee. The committee was charged with examining the Republican delegate selection process and make recommendations for the 1972 convention. Their recommendations included:

1. Ensuring an equal number of male and female delegates in each state convention.
2. Establishing a quota for delegates under 25 years of age.
3. Maintaining a required level of minority membership on the four standing committees of the national conventions.

As a consequence of these two committees, delegate selection for the conventions has become more democratic and more demographically representative. Party bosses no longer have the same influence that they used to.

Today, conventions perform the following functions:

1. Formally nominate the president and vice president.
2. Serve as the party's highest policy-making organ.
3. Adopt a party platform.

Vice President

While the nomination of the president is virtually sewn up by the time the conventions roll around, the choice for vice president is usually not made known until the convention or shortly before. This was the case with [George W.] Bush's recent selection of Dick Cheney. Delaying the choice of a running-mate is a commonly used strategy to build public excitement and anticipation for the convention.

Since national conventions only occur every four years, party leaders and delegates use this time to discuss rules that govern the party. In off convention years, parties are governed by the national committees, the Democratic National Committee (DNC), and the Republican National Committee

(RNC). During meetings they can adopt new rules and discuss the concerns of the party at the state level.

Party Platforms

Parties will also adopt a party platform. These platforms are made public during the conventions and highlight key policy issues and positions that each party stands for. Many of these issues include salient positions on topics such as abortion and taxes. Party member may be divided on some issues. For example, while Republicans have opted for a pro-life platform, some party members support a pro-choice position.

In any event, the primary goal of conventions is to help unify the party and present itself in the best light possible before the general elections in November. To show a unified front, conventions are often highly scripted. This may account for some of the public's recent lack of interest in conventions. Still, the public can count on hearing from some of the nation's most prominent political figures during prime time key note addresses.

VIEWPOINT 4

> *"Political conventions are glitzy affairs where the party faithful formally pick their White House contender [as well as being] venues for sumptuous private parties where lobbyists and lawmakers meet."*

National Conventions Have Become Fundraising Tools for Political Parties

Fredreka Schouten

Political conventions have increasingly become a forum to attract financial contributions for political parties, Fredreka Schouten argues in the following viewpoint. Schouten describes efforts to limit the donations given to conventions and provides details on how large contributions are made to parties to support the nomination gatherings. She points out that contributions to conventions are not limited by federal law, unlike other forms of campaign donations, and reports on some hefty funds given for the 2008 conventions. Schouten is a journalist who writes for USA Today, *a daily national newspaper.*

As you read, consider the following questions:

1. What is the key difference between contributions to political campaigns and donations to political conventions, according to Schouten?
2. What was the 2007 legislation that attempted to limit contributions for conventions, as cited by the author?
3. What do companies seek to gain by contributing to conventions, in Schouten's opinion?

Ethics rules approved by Congress to curb lobbyists' influence did little to change a key way they curry favor with lawmakers: underwriting the national conventions where presidential nominees are picked.

A bill ... unveiled in the House of Representatives [on January 29, 2007] would limit lawmakers' ability to raise money from special interests for conventions but would not affect the 2008 events. A Senate bill passed [in January 2007] would bar members from attending lobbyist-sponsored parties thrown in their honor but would leave intact the ability of special interests to pay for the quadrennial events.

Money and Conventions

The host committee in Denver, where Democrats will gather [in 2008], already has collected more than $16 million, some from companies lobbying Congress and federal agencies. Organizers in Minneapolis-St. Paul, site of the Republican event, also raise money from companies with business in Washington.

Paying for conventions "is a way in which these interests can buy undue influence," said Fred Wertheimer, president of non-partisan watchdog group, Democracy 21.

Federal rules do not limit the source or amount of convention donations. Names of donors don't have to be made public until the events are over. By contrast, campaign contributions to candidates from individuals are capped at $2.300

The 2007 Presidential Funding Act

'(1) IN GENERAL- Any person ... shall not solicit, receive, direct, transfer, or spend any funds in connection with a presidential nominating convention of any political party, including funds for a host committee, civic committee, municipality, or any other person or entity spending funds in connection with such a convention, unless such funds—

'(A) are not in excess of the amounts permitted with respect to contributions to the political committee established and maintained by a national political party committee ... and

'(B) are not from a source prohibited by this Act from making contributions in connection with an election for Federal office.

'(2) EXCEPTION- Paragraph (1) shall not apply to—

'(A) payments by a Federal, State, or local government if the funds used for the payments are from the general public tax revenues of such government and are not derived from donations made to a State or local government for purposes of any convention; and

'(B) payments by any person for the purpose of promoting the suitability of a city as a convention site in advance of its selection, welcoming convention attendees to the city, or providing shopping or entertainment guides to convention attendees.'

U.S. House of Representatives, 110th Congress, January 2007.

per election, while political action committees of unions and companies are limited to $5,000.

Political conventions are glitzy affairs where the party faithful formally pick their White House contender. They also are venues for sumptuous private parties where lobbyists and lawmakers meet.

At the 2004 GOP [Republican] convention, the American Gas Association staged parties honoring lawmakers, including a "Wildcatter's Ball", for Sen. James Inhofe, R-Okla., then-chairman of the Senate committee that regulates the industry. Under the Senate bill, Inhofe would be banned from attending the event.

Reps. Marty Meehan, D-Mass., Christopher Shays, R-Conn. and David Price, D-N.C., introduce[d] the bill that would bar lawmakers and federal candidates from soliciting donations to pay for the conventions. [The bill was titled the Presidential Funding Act of 2007.]

Influence and Contributions

Xcel Energy, an electricity and natural gas company with plants in eight states, is giving $1.5 million to each convention. The company spent nearly $2.5 million on Washington lobbying in 2005, the last full year for which data are available, according to the Center for Responsive Politics, a non-partisan group that tracks lobbying cash.

Among Xcel's battles: an unsuccessful attempt to exclude the power plants it operates in West Texas from federal rules to reduce air pollution in Eastern states.

Cyndi Lesher of the Twin Cities convention host committee said her company and others give "in the spirit of a great civic event."

Lesher is also chief executive of an Xcel subsidiary, Northern States Power. The St. Paul arena where the Republican convention will take place bears Xcel's name.

"I'm not naive. It does help for people to know the names of these companies," she said. "Do these companies think they can buy influence? That has not been my experience."

Telecommunications giant Qwest has pledged $6 million to each convention. Steve Davis, the company's vice president for public policy, said the sponsorship is not politically motivated, but represents a chance to market Qwest.

"Anytime one meets with a politician, there are opportunities to raise issues," Davis said, "but for us, these are business opportunities."

Cable giant Comcast has pledged $5 million to the Democratic convention, according to Steve Farber, co-chairman of Denver's host committee.

Comcast spokeswoman Sena Fitzmaurice said the company will support both conventions. She declined to comment further.

"The fact they wrote a check for $6 million or $1 million or a $100,000, I don't think its going to accelerate getting a phone call returned any quicker," Farber said.

He said the first political convention in Denver in a century is a "phenomenal" economic opportunity for the city and Colorado.

In 2005, Qwest spent more than $3.4 million on federal lobbying and Comcast spent nearly $4 million, according to the Center for Responsive Politics.

Both companies oppose "net neutrality" bills in Congress that would bar them from charging customers higher prices for videos and other content transmitted over high-speed Internet connections.

VIEWPOINT 5

> *"Early-primary states have an enhanced role in vetting candidates."*

Earlier Primaries Improve the Nomination Process

Marie Price

Iowa and New Hampshire have traditionally played an overly influential role in the presidential nomination process because they hold an early primary or caucus. In the following viewpoint Marie Price examines arguments in favor of and opposed to early primaries among all of the states as they are expressed by a number of leading scholars. Price is a reporter for the Oklahoma City newspaper the Journal Record.

As you read, consider the following questions:

1. How has New Hampshire responded to the efforts by other states to hold their primaries earlier in the year, according to Price?
2. How would a shortened primary season affect fundraising by candidates, in the author's opinion?
3. According to Price, does the current system force candidates to focus on one state or on many simultaneously?

Marie Price, "Earlier Primaries Changing Presidential Race," *Journal Record* (Oklahoma City, OK), February 5, 2007.

The fact that California, Florida, New Jersey, Illinois and other larger states want to move their presidential primaries up to early February of [2008] has political experts scratching their heads over how this will impact an already tight election season. Oklahoma and some other small states are scheduled to hold their presidential primaries on Feb. 5, [2008].

The rush to hold earlier primaries reportedly has "first-at-all-costs" New Hampshire officials considering moving up their presidential contest, perhaps before Jan. 1. Only Iowa's caucuses come earlier than the New Hampshire primary. "Everybody's front-loading," said University of Oklahoma political science professor Keith Gaddie. "It's always an effort to increase your influence in determining who the presidential nominee will be." Gaddie said early-primary states have an enhanced role in vetting candidates. "What happens in these early primaries dictates who gets to go forward and who doesn't," he said. "Momentum can be established by a candidate in an early primary, then they can build on it."

Gaddie said front-loading has been a reality since the late 1980s, when Southern states got together in "Super Tuesday" primaries to increase their influence on the process. "With all of these major states front-loading, it really diminishes the influence of the Oklahoma primary," said Gaddie. "People just aren't going to pay attention as much, because our delegate count is so small." On the other hand, he said, Oklahoma may draw candidates who think they can win here, such as former Democratic U.S. Sen. John Edwards and former Arkansas Gov. Mike Huckabee, a Republican. Previously, he said, that first Tuesday in February brought more presidential candidates into states like Oklahoma and South Carolina. "Having a highly competitive primary like that is really good for your activist base, because it gets them interested," Gaddie said. Presidential primaries have reduced the influence of national political parties on the nomination system.

Early Primaries Benefit Minority Voters

Until recently, it was the largely homogenous, disproportionately rural Iowa and New Hampshire that had the biggest say in the nominating process, which meant that many other constituencies with divergent interests had little voice in determining the parties' nominees.

Now that many states with diverse populations and larger urban centers are joining the fray, that has changed. For example, while there has been some note taken of the increased role African Americans will play in the early South Carolina Democratic contest, there has been little discussion of the potential influence of the African American electorate on the primaries more broadly. Also largely unaddressed to date is that having more urban voters participating earlier might have a great impact on the content of campaign debate and primary outcomes....

Among the states that expect to have nominating contests on or before February 5 are Nevada, California, New Mexico, New Jersey, Texas, and New York. All of these states have significant Latino populations, and therefore Latinos have a greater potential than ever to influence the outcomes of the nomination process for both parties

Tova Andrea Wang, Century Foundation Issue Brief, *April 11, 2007.*

Party Politics

Gaddie said the Democrats have tried to assert some control by putting in place rules to punish candidates and parties that defy a schedule laid out by the party. However, he said that schedule allows state parties to schedule primaries beginning Feb. 5, 2008. "The time is now to start building organizations for these early primaries, because you really need a year," Gaddie said. With a $100 million price tag cited for a viable presidential campaign, the shortened political season makes fundraising more vital than ever. "It puts Clinton and Obama on the Democratic side in the driver's seat, because they have large sources of money," Gaddie said. Those types of candidates will go after the big delegate-count states, he said. Candidates with less ability to raise funds must be more strategic, Gaddie said. In Democratic primaries, he said, a candidate need not come in first in order to garner a proportionate share of delegates. He said Republicans, in winner-take-all contests, must look for states where they can win. Oklahoma Republican Party Chairman Tom Daxon said presidential primaries give voters the chance to scrutinize front-runners like U.S. Sen. John McCain, R-Ariz., and former New York Mayor Rudy Giuliani. "While I don't like the way a lot of that is often done, in the overall scheme of things, it's probably a good thing, at the end of the day, that we do have that kind of scrutiny," he said. Daxon said that with early primaries, someone will invariably step forward in, say, New Hampshire, and do better than everyone expects. "I have no idea who that's going to be," he said. Daxon said that could improve the chances for candidates such as U.S. Sen. Sam Brownback, R-Kans. or U.S. Rep. Duncan Hunter, R-Calif., who would also undergo intense scrutiny. "By the time you get to your convention, your guy is pretty well vetted," he said. If every state had its primary around the same time, Daxon said, there might not be enough time for all that to happen. Daxon said a more compressed, expensive political calendar could make it more difficult for dark horse candidates to get in the race. "You're going to have to raise a substantial amount of money, if you're going to be a serious candidate for president," he said. "The current system allows somebody the luxury of focusing on a handful of races, if not even a single race, with the prospect of doing well, and then leveraging that into the kind of support they need to really go national. If you compress that time period, I think you've got some issues."

Problems for Minor Candidates

Former Oklahoma U.S. Sen. Fred Harris, now a political science professor at the University of New Mexico, has also run for president himself, and once chaired the Democratic National Committee. "I think it really makes it much more difficult for lesser-known and lesser-financed candidates to get a real hearing," Harris said of the squeezed presidential primary season. In the past, Harris said, candidates were elected through "retail politics," by person-to-person, shake-one-hand-at-a-time campaigning. "That system made it possible for a lesser-known candidate, a lesser-financed candidate, to emerge," he said. That type of campaigning helped nominate Georgia Gov. Jimmy Carter and Arkansas Gov. Bill Clinton as their party's candidates, both of whom were "way down in the polls" to start with, he said. "You didn't have to be highly popular nationwide or well-known nationwide, or have all of your money up front," he said. "If you did well in the early contests, the national standing and additional money would come".

The Impact of Large States

If delegate-rich states such as California move up their primaries, [Harris] said, it will be very difficult for less well-known candidates to surface. "We will really constrict the choices that people have," Harris said. This doesn't necessarily mean that candidates will start giving states like Oklahoma a complete pass, he said. "Any serious candidate is going to have to run everywhere, no matter what," Harris said. "But the spotlight and the emphasis on the lesser-populated states are going to be diluted." Top-tier candidates do need to raise about $100 million, he said. "But you didn't have to do all of that at once," Harris added. "Now, with California and New Jersey in there, you're going to have to have most of your money pretty much up front." Harris said the current system allows voters to winnow down the list of potential candidates. "Now, there will be a kind of national-popularity and campaign-financing primary that will winnow them out long before these first contests," he said. Harris said, "We should just leave well enough alone," but doesn't think that will be the case. After the 2008 contests, he said, the process may see the establishment of a sequence of primaries and caucuses set up by party regulations.

Harris said some have suggested changing either to a national primary or at most four regional contests, both of which he opposes. "It would limit the choices voters would have," he said. "There would be a great number of people that just couldn't get started."

Viewpoint 6

> "Iowa and New Hampshire are profoundly unrepresentative of America as a whole."

Earlier Primaries Give Unfair Advantages to Some States

Cullen Murphy

The results of the Iowa caucus and New Hampshire primary are often criticized for being unrepresentative of the other states, argues Cullen Murphy in the following viewpoint. Murphy explores the problems with early primaries and caucuses as he searches for the perfect state to hold the first primary. He concludes with his choice as the best first primary state. Cullen Murphy has been the managing editor of the Atlantic Monthly *and is the author of* The Word According to Eve: Women and the Bible in Ancient Times and Our Own.

As you read, consider the following questions:

1. What are the major criticisms of Iowa and New Hampshire having the first caucus and primary in the nation, as cited by Murphy?
2. Which state is statistically representative of the United States, in the author's opinion?

Cullen Murphy, "Primary Considerations," *Atlantic Monthly*, vol. 293, issue 3, April 2004, pp. 148–149. www.theatlantic.com.

3. Why does Murphy argue that the first primary should be in Missouri?

The [2004] presidential-primary season is now behind us, mostly, and the quadrennial hand-wringing has begun over the prominent roles played by the Iowa caucuses and the New Hampshire primary. It's not surprising, of course, that the candidates who fared poorly in these early contests would suddenly realize that Iowa and New Hampshire are profoundly unrepresentative of America as a whole. Iowans on average are more literate than the typical American, and they get divorced far less frequently. New Hampshire is tiny, rural, white, fickle, and flinty. Sheesh! If only they'd known!

Criticism of Iowa and New Hampshire

But it's not just the losing candidates who weigh in.... The litany of complaint grows longer with every presidential cycle. The columnist William Safire almost a decade ago called the New Hampshire primary a "media-saturated joke"; the state's citizens, he went on, are "overexposed, over-polled, over-campaigned upon." *The New York Times*, arguing recently for the creation of a "more thoughtful process," noted that there is nothing "historically sacred" about Iowa's "icicle-festooned precinct scrums." Appearing on *The Capital Gang*, Kate O'Beirne, the Washington editor of *National Review*, remarked, "The Iowa caucuses measure something. They sure don't measure the national appeal of a candidate." *The San Diego Union-Tribune*, published in a mighty state that has played no serious role in the presidential nominating process in two generations, was scornful of Iowa and New Hampshire. "They are such small states," an editorial observed in January [2004]. "In fact, with 2.9 million residents last year, Iowa was no more populous than San Diego County. With 1.2 million residents, New Hampshire was no more populous than the city of San Diego." The former senator Slade Gorton, of Washington, has sonorously declared that "nonsensical traditions of presiden-

tial candidates posing for photographs in Iowa cornfields and eating doughnuts in New Hampshire diners are not a proper manner in which to select the leader of the free world"—a sentiment embraced by Senator Joseph Lieberman, of Connecticut, until he himself decided to compete in New Hampshire (and perhaps embraced by him once again, in the wake of his abysmal showing in that contest).

A few days after the [2004] New Hampshire vote, the chairman of the Democratic National Committee, Terry McAuliffe, provided an opening for sharp criticism of the selection process when he put New Hampshire on notice, explaining that it had better vote Democratic in 2004 if it wanted to retain its first-in-the-nation presidential primary. The predictable cries of outrage from New Hampshire politicians and editorial writers were met by huzzahs from elected officials in Michigan and Pennsylvania, who pointed out that their states are considerably more reflective of America's diversity than the Granite State is.

Regional Primaries

The skepticism about Iowa and New Hampshire has its merits, no doubt, and when the national election is over, we'll hear about ideas for reforming the selection process. Someone will again propose a series of regional primaries. Someone will again suggest that the state with the highest voter turnout be allowed to hold the first primary next time. Maybe the honor of first-in-the-nation primary should henceforward be awarded alphabetically, starting with Alabama in 2008 and moving to Wyoming two centuries later. And so on.

But a central background question remains on the table. If Iowa and New Hampshire are unrepresentative of America (as obviously they are), then what is the most representative state? Michigan and Pennsylvania may be "more" representative than Iowa or New Hampshire, but are they *utterly* representative? If we had to select one state to stand for America in all its parts—the state you'd transplant to Mars to make sure our starter colony grew up just like the country we have here—which one would it be?

The Perfect State

If you start simply with core demographic characteristics, the answer is Illinois. The United States is 75.1 percent white, 12.5 percent Hispanic, 12.3 percent African-American, 3.6 percent Asian, and 0.9 percent Native American. The respective figures for Illinois are 73.5, 12.3, 15.1, 3.4, and 0.2. But a number of other states, though not quite so close on every measure, can lay claim to "ballpark" status on diversity: Florida, Michigan, Missouri, New Jersey, Pennsylvania, and Texas. And if you pick different data, different states emerge on top. When it comes to the urban-rural ratio, for instance, the U.S. average is 79 to 21. That's matched pretty closely by Texas and Pennsylvania. If you look at certain economic indices, Missouri emerges as fairly representative, with 12 percent of its work force in manufacturing (as compared with 11.7 nationwide) and 13.5 percent in labor unions (also 13.5 percent nationwide). Some 25 percent of all businesses in Missouri are owned by women; the figure for the country as a whole is 26 percent.

Some winnowing out is in order. Fortunately, most of these states have some disqualifying characteristic. Texas, by its own boastful admission, is not like the rest of the country; and indeed, it used to be independent. Florida, with no stable intrinsic character, suffers from dangerous weather and a skewed population structure; any reader of [Florida novelist] Carl Hiaasen understands that Florida is an outlier. Michigan's one major metropolis is in a state of inexorable decay. New Jersey consists essentially of suburbs, and as a media market is a dependency of Philadelphia or New York. Pennsylvania is surprisingly inert, economically and demographically. Illinois is just too flat—it lacks the highlander element that so often provides a kind of cultural ballast.

Missouri

Which leaves Missouri, at the geographical heart of the continent, a state that straddled North and South during the Civil War and has straddled East and West since the days of Lewis and Clark. It's the state that gave us Harry Truman *and* John Ashcroft, Dick Gregory *and* Rush Limbaugh, Josephine Baker *and* Burt Bacharach. The population of an "average" American state (total U.S. population divided by fifty) would be about 5.7 million; Missouri's is 5.6 million. The average state of the Union has 10.7 electoral votes; Missouri has eleven. The average state is 74,000 square miles; Missouri is 70,000. In the continental United States the average state with a coast has some 400 miles of coastline; if you count the Mississippi River (which is, after all, managed by the U.S. Coast Guard), Missouri has about the same. The people of Missouri have a distinctive manner of speech, but it's not the easily caricatured speech of Boston or New York or southern California or the

South, or the affectless tones of the hyper-educated—it's closer to what foreigners think of as an "American" accent.

Spend some time crunching the numbers on Missouri, and here are some of the things you'll find:

	Missouri	*U.S. avg.*
Mobile homes as % of housing	8.2	7.6
% population under age 18	25.5	25.7
% high school graduates	81.3	80.4
% over 24 with 4 yrs. college	26.7	26.7
Cesarean births (per 100)	22.1	22.0
Infant-mortality rate (per 1,000 live births)	7.2	6.9
% low-birth-weight babies	7.6	7.6
% in same house five years	53.6	54.1
% below poverty line	11.7	12.4
Retail sales per capita	$9,482	$9,190
Persons per square mile	81.2	79.6
Travel time to work (min.)	23.8	25.5
% children with Internet access	52.0	48.0
% children with no home phone	3.0	3.0
Hypothermia-related deaths (per 100,000)	0.2	0.3
Federal aid to state and local government (per capita)	$1,258	$1,233

That looks like a match to me. It may be worth noting that for more than a century in presidential contests Missouri has gone the way of the winning candidate more than any other state. Since 1900 it has voted "wrong" only once, in 1956. The *Almanac of American Politics* offers an observation that strikes me as a clincher: "An imaginary, flat map of the United States population, if everyone weighed the same, would balance near Edgar Springs in Phelps County, Missouri."

Periodical Bibliography

The following articles have been selected to supplement the diverse views presented in this chapter.

Paul Bedard	"Washington Whispers," *U.S. News & World Report*, May 21, 2007.
Ari Berman	"Making Elections Fair," *Nation*, April 30, 2007.
Craig Crawford	"Get Ready to Rumble!" *CQ Weekly*, November 20, 2006.
Raymond Fischer	"The Amazing Race Is On," *USA Today* magazine, May 2007.
Emily Goodin	"Compression Season," *National Journal*, January 27, 2007.
Kenneth Jost	"Electing the President?" *CQ Researcher*, April 20, 2007.
David D. Perlmutter	"Political Blogs: The New Iowa?" *Chronicle of Higher Education*, May 26, 2006.
Andrew Romano	"Here Comes ... 'Super-Duper Tuesday,'" *Newsweek*, March 26, 2007.
Mark Wegner	"Levin Tries Again to Change Presidential Primary Process," *CongressDaily*, March 15, 2007.
Laurence Whitehead	"The Challenge of Closely Fought Elections," *Journal of Democracy*, April 2007.

OPPOSING VIEWPOINTS® SERIES

Chapter 2

Should Campaign Spending Be Limited?

Chapter Preface

Running for political office in the United States is expensive. The average member of the House of Representatives has to spend more than $1 million every two years in congressional campaigns. Senators spend more than $6 million every six years. In the 2004 presidential campaign, Republican George W. Bush, who won the election, spent more than $258 million. Bush's opponent, Democrat John Kerry, spent over $233 million.

In the United States, presidential campaigns are financed by a mixture of public and private financing. During the primaries and caucuses, presidential candidates who raise at least $5,000 in twenty different states are given matching funds, up to $250 per contribution by the federal government. In return, they must agree to limit their private fundraising and their overall expenditures to no more than $20 million. If a party's candidate received at least 5 percent of the vote in the last presidential election, the government provides financial support for that party's nominating convention. In 2004 the government gave the Democratic Party and the Republican Party more than $14 million each for their conventions. Once a party that reached the 5 percent threshold in the previous election has chosen a candidate, the government provides funds for its campaign. In 2004 it gave Bush and Kerry over $74 million for their campaigns. This money comes from individual income-tax returns where citizens choose the option to have $3 of their taxes go to support campaign financing. On average, only about 8 percent of Americans take this option.

As campaigns have become more expensive, candidates have had to rely more and more on private funds. In the 2008 presidential primaries, most of the major candidates, including Hillary Clinton, John McCain, Barack Obama, and Rudy

Giuliani have declined public funds for their campaigns so that they can raise more private dollars. Many perceive that this emphasis on money forces the candidates to cater to the rich. As Jay Mandle summarizes, "When electoral campaigns are paid for by the rich, the substance of politics is confined to the issues and policies that wealthy funders approve of."

In the following chapter, authors explore the benefits and problems of the current system of funding presidential elections. They analyze the utility of public campaign financing and various reform proposals in an effort to discern the most effective and inclusive system to pay for presidential elections.

VIEWPOINT 1

> *"Should only the rich, or those who can talk the rich into giving them money, have the chance to run for office?"*

Campaign Financing Needs to Be Reformed

Public Agenda

One of the major problems in the modern American presidential election process is the enormous cost of the campaigns. In the following viewpoint, the research organization Public Agenda provides an overview of the main loopholes in current campaign finance laws and of efforts to reform the system. The author also examines the reactions of the major parties, as well as of the American public, to the reform initiatives. Public Agenda is a nonpartisan organization that analyzes domestic policies and produces reports designed to educate Americans.

As you read, consider the following questions:

1. What is "soft money," as explained by Public Agenda?
2. How did politicians attempt to influence voters during the 1700s, according to the author?

Public Agenda, "Campaign Reform: Overview," *PublicAgenda.org*, March 27, 2007.

3. What have been the major campaign finance reforms in the 2000s, as reported by Public Agenda?

When money changes hands in politics, a cloud of suspicion rises. Now so much money is changing hands—upwards of $3 billion in a presidential election year—the cloud never lifts. Running for office is an expensive proposition, particularly for president or for statewide offices like governor or senator, but the amounts that have changed hands in recent years are staggering.

Presidential and congressional candidates spent a combined total of $3 billion on the 2000 elections, compared to $2.2 billion in 1996 and $1.8 billion in 1992, according to the Center for Responsive Politics, a nonpartisan group that focuses on fund raising and its effects on public policy. In the 2000 presidential contest, George W. Bush received $193 million and spent $185 million, while Al Gore received $133 million and spent $120 million—and those figures don't include the large sums of "soft money" raised by parties to indirectly support a candidate. Bush's total expenditure, a record for a presidential run, is all the more striking given that, unlike Gore, he chose to forgo public funding during the primary to avoid federal spending limits. Gore received $83 million in federal funds for the primary and general election campaigns, and Bush, who accepted public funding in the general election, received $67 million.

Large though those numbers are, campaign finance spending is only part of the problem of money and politics. Year-in and year-out, corporations and interest groups spend millions to kill legislation or obtain tax breaks and favored treatment in laws and regulations. In Washington, D.C., alone, more than $1.4 billion a year is spent on efforts to influence federal officials. There are 38 registered lobbyists and $2.7 million in lobbying money for each member of Congress. And that doesn't even cover lobbying done at the state level.

With all that money floating around, the natural question is what (or who) is being bought? Corporations and interest groups who give money say what they're most interested in is "access"—that giving money increases their chances of being listened to when their cause is being debated in Congress. Sometimes, also, wealthy people give in order to promote ideas they're interested in, such as when Ross Perot spent his own money to run for president, or the way billionaire George Soros funds ballot referendums to change drug laws. Many critics of campaign-finance reform plans argue that there's nothing wrong with groups of like-minded people getting together to elect candidates who agree with them, and to lobby them once they're in office.

Campaign Fundraising History

But that raises another question. Most Americans don't give money to political candidates, and less than one-tenth of 1 percent give more than $1,000. Should only the rich, or those who can talk the rich into giving them money, have the chance to run for office? Should wealthy funders be, if not the only ones to be heard on public policy issues, the loudest?

Democracy's most persistent dilemma may be that politicians need lots of money to publicize their candidacy, engage citizens, and get voters to the polls—all without appearing to buy votes or show favor to financial supporters. When George Washington first "stood" for Virginia's colonial legislature in 1757, it was common to lure voters to the polls with food and drink. But Washington was accused of trying to buy the election by providing 160 gallons of rum, wine and beer to influence a mere 391 registered voters. Twenty years later, James Madison personally tried to reform the system by not distributing liquor to voters, and was defeated for re-election to the Virginia legislature.

In the 19th Century, politicians would openly shake down government contractors for contributions, and until 1883 it was legal to require federal workers to contribute time and money to their party in order to keep their jobs. Those practices, and the then-stunning cost of elections (the 1896 presidential race between William McKinley and William Jennings Bryan cost $7 million, or more than $140 million in current dollars when adjusted for inflation, according to Economic History Services) led to a series of reforms. Some were aimed at controlling money: in 1907 corporate contributions were banned, and laws requiring candidate campaign disclosures were passed in 1910 and 1925. Other changes were aimed at distributing power in new ways, hopefully less vulnerable to influence, such as initiative and referendum laws allowing voters to directly approve legislation and recall petitions to remove officeholders.

Still, the cost of campaigning continued to rise, particularly in the 1950s and '60s as candidates became increasingly reliant on television advertising as a campaign tool. In 1971, Congress passed the Federal Elections Campaign Act which regulated campaign spending and mandated disclosure of contributions. In 1974, after the Watergate scandal forced President Nixon to resign from office, Congress produced the most comprehensive campaign-reform legislation ever. The law strengthened disclosure requirements, set new limits on contributions and spending, established a system of public financing for presidential elections, and created an independent agency—the Federal Election Commission [FEC]—to enforce the new rules.

In 1976, though, the Supreme Court rejected part of the 1974 law with its ruling in *Buckley v. Valeo*. The court ruled that limits on individual contributions were a constitutional way to deter corruption but it struck down limits on candidates' campaign spending, ruling that such limits would violate their right to free speech. The only exception, the court added, was that candidates could accept voluntary limits on their campaign spending in exchange for public funds. Public

The Main Reforms of the McCain-Feingold Bill

National parties and congressional committees may only raise and spend hard money contributions received from individuals and political action committees ("PACs"): no labor or corporate contributions are permitted. This soft-money ban is the bedrock of the McCain-Feingold bill. National parties and congressional committees also are banned from making contributions to non-profit organizations.

State parties are required to use hard-money contributions to fund get-out-the-vote ("GOTV") or voter registration drives in the 120 days preceding an election, or any other activities designed to influence a federal election during an election year (even-numbered year). A $10,000 individual contribution exception is made for specified state party activities. Candidates are banned from raising soft money for GOTV, voter registration, and other federal election activities.

Brookings Institution, 2007.

financing systems, where tax dollars are offered as an inducement to limit spending, are now in place for presidential elections and in some states.

Soft Money, Hard Choices

Despite the efforts at reform, the amount of money spent on elections continues to grow. Over the last decade, much of the focus has been on "soft money," the unlimited and nearly unregulated donations made to political parties that can then be used for activities on behalf of candidates. The Center for Responsive Politics estimates the Democratic and Republican parties raised nearly a half-billion dollars in soft money for the 2000 election. And even during 2001, an off-year for federal elections, Democratic and Republican party leaders estimate they raised $151 million in soft-money contributions—a 50 percent increase over 1999, the last comparable year, according to Common Cause, a nonpartisan group that studies political fund raising.

The "soft money" loophole grew out of a 1979 amendment to the campaign-finance law. Ironically, the 1974 law had banned soft money, and party activists complained that they couldn't raise enough money for routine activities like buying bumper stickers and "get-out-the-vote" efforts. Congress amended the law to allow state and local parties to spend unlimited amounts of money on campaign materials to promote federal candidates. In practice, though, it has become the primary method of raising millions of dollars from wealthy contributors for presidential and congressional candidates.

Another focus has been on so-called "issue ads." Under the law, nonprofit organizations formed to advocate for a specific cause or issue can raise money and run ads to promote it. That includes running ads that attack candidates who oppose the advocacy group's cause, with no oversight at all, so long as they don't coordinate their efforts with a candidate or say in so many words to vote for or against someone. Some of the toughest attack ads come from these organizations, which often have ambiguous names that don't reveal who they really are.

Reform Efforts

In recent years, legislation to ban soft money—most famously the McCain-Feingold bill—has stalled in Congress. [In 2007], though, in the wake of the Enron scandal, Congress did pass a version of the McCain-Feingold legislation which bars national parties from raising soft money and prevents state parties from using soft money for issue ads. But it also doubles the limit on "hard money" contributions directly to candidates to $2,000. Critics say the law has already been watered down by the FEC in its regulations to enforce the soft-money ban.

The legislation also prohibits unions, corporations and nonprofit groups from running issue ads aimed at a candidate on television or radio within 30 days of a primary or within 60 days of a general election. The law would take effect Nov. 6 [2007], a day after the next congressional elections. Opponents have already filed suit, saying the law infringes on freedom of speech. The opposition is made up of an unlikely combination of groups, including the AFL-CIO [labor organization], the American Civil Liberties Union, the U.S. Chamber of Commerce and the Christian Coalition.

What's more, some skeptics suggest that special interests would simply find new loopholes to exploit, much as they did with soft money. And the issue ads won't go away altogether: The Shays-Meehan bill still allows them to be used in telephone and direct-mail campaigns.

Meanwhile, Democratic and Republican party leaders aren't taking any chances. House approval of Shays-Meehan has prompted a flurry of fund-raising appeals to big contributors. The message: Write that big check now before the door slams shut on soft money.

Public Opinion

In recent years, surveys have shown strong public support for an overhaul of campaign-finance laws. Surveys show more than half of Americans say elections are for sale to whoever has the most money, and a majority say high campaign costs discourage good people from running for office.

Yet, when surveys ask Americans to rank the issues that are most important to them, campaign-finance reform is rated much lower than other concerns, such as education and the economy. And, in a recent survey, fewer than half of Americans said they considered campaign-finance reform an important legislative priority.

So if the system needs fixing so badly, why isn't the topic more important to voters? Perhaps people doubt that technical changes in the fund-raising process would improve politicians' moral behavior or reduce the influence of special interests. More than half of Americans now say that they trust politicians in Washington only "some of the time" or "none of the time," and the reasons they give include a belief that politicians lie and are only out to get what they can for themselves.

The public is also unsure as to what reforms should be introduced. For example, majorities favor banning soft money and limiting individual contributions to political parties, but 40 percent say enforcing existing laws should be enough. Nearly six in 10 oppose public financing of elections.

Viewpoint 2

> "The current U.S. system of campaign financing blends the philosophies of reformers, defenders of the existing system, and the judicial rulings ... on government regulation."

The Current Campaign Financing System Effectively Balances Many Interests

Joseph E. Cantor

Although the amount of money spent on presidential elections in the United States is often criticized, Joseph E. Cantor argues in the following viewpoint that contemporary finance laws create a balance among many different interests in American society. Cantor also explores the history of campaign finance in the United States, including major Supreme Court decisions on the subject. Cantor is a policy analyst for the Congressional Research Service, where he advises members of Congress on campaign finance law.

As you read, consider the following questions:

1. What are the main sources of campaign donations for candidates in the United States, according to Cantor?

Joseph E. Cantor, "The State of Campaign Finance," *Elections 2004*, United States Department of State, September 2003. http://usinfo.state.gov.

2. What was the significance of the 1976 Supreme Court decision, *Buckley v. Valeo*, in the author's opinion?
3. According to Cantor, what three principles guide federal campaign law in the United States?

A prominent American politician once declared that "money is the mother's milk of politics." This is hardly surprising given that America's democratic form of government is based on free and open elections and a tradition of pluralism whereby competing interests vie to influence public policy. That characterization is especially apt today, as the size of the electorate necessitates reliance at least in elections for major office on mass media to communicate with voters. Broadcast time is an efficient but costly means of reaching mass audiences.

Campaign Contributions

Candidates for public office in the United States typically rely on four sources for campaign funds: (1) individual citizens who make direct contributions; (2) their own political parties; (3) interest groups, often through political action committees (PACs); and (4) their personal and family resources. A fifth source—public funds—has also been available in some elections, most notably presidential elections, since the 1970s.

Growing reliance on the broadcast media and the professionalization of politics have led to increasingly costly election campaigns. Candidates for the presidency spent $607 million in the 2000 presidential election, while candidates for Congress spent just over $1 billion. The average winning candidate for the U.S. Senate spent $7.4 million that year, and the average winning candidate for the U.S. House of Representatives, $849,000. Spending by candidates, however, increasingly constitutes less and less of total expenditures to influence elections, as parties and interest groups play a greater role in direct voter communication.

Traditionally, political parties and interest groups focused their resources on monetary contributions to candidates, who spent money on voter contact, both to persuade voters through advertisements, mailings, etc. and to ensure that voters get to the polls to cast their ballots. In contemporary elections, political parties and interest groups both contribute to favored candidates and spend money more directly to maximize their own influence on the election outcome. This phenomenon makes it harder to monitor the flow of money in elections, and it has presented policy-makers with particular challenges in seeking to regulate money outside the direct control of candidates.

The Current System

Critics have long asserted that high spending in U.S. elections, combined with the reliance for funds on private sources, raises concerns about possible undue influence over public policy by wealthy donors and interests. Proposed solutions generally involve greater government regulation of money in politics, beginning with improved transparency to facilitate public awareness of election financing and to thus inhibit "special interests" from obstructing the perceived "public interest." "Reformers" have been opposed by those who see election spending as proportionate with both the costs of goods and services in today's economy and the size of government budgets. These observers see election spending as the price a democracy pays for electoral competition, with large contributions and expenditures by interest groups as the contemporary expression of America's long-standing pluralism. The judicial branch of government often raises another issue involved in regulating campaign funding—whether restrictions on campaign giving and spending unduly limit donors' constitutionally protected right to free speech in the political arena.

It might be said that the current U.S. system of campaign financing blends the philosophies of reformers, defenders of the existing system, and the judicial rulings that have set parameters on government regulation. It reflects both the laws that have been enacted—and upheld—and the way in which American politics has evolved.

Candidate-Centered Elections

Comparisons of the American system of election financing with those of other democracies can help us understand some unique aspects of the U.S. political system.

First and foremost is America's departure from the parliamentary system used in most democracies, which places political parties at the center of the process of electing and then running the government. While parties play an important role in American elections, they are far less important than earlier in history, before the many reforms and other changes that occurred during the 20th century.

The United States has, for better or worse, a candidate-centered, rather than party-centered, electoral system. Candidates tend to be independent agents who do not owe their careers or nominations to party officials, but rather to primary election voters. While this independence has had certain salutary effects in terms of greater openness and accountability, it has undoubtedly added to election costs, as candidates need quasi-independent campaign machinery and funding sources. Likewise, many contemporary voters pride themselves on being independent of party labels, voting "for the person, not the party," and thus placing a further burden on the candidate to communicate effectively as a public figure.

First Amendment

Another unique aspect of the U.S. system is the strong role in political processes of the well-defined rights of free speech and association guaranteed under the First Amendment to the U.S. Constitution. It is the judiciary's role to decide whether enacted statutes are in conflict with those rights. In its landmark 1976 ruling—*Buckley v. Valeo*—the U.S. Supreme Court overturned limitations on amounts that campaigns, political parties, and interest groups could spend to communicate with voters, while permitting restrictions on sources of funds to entities involved in elections. The Court declared that limitations on expenditures to communicate with voters constituted an impermissible restriction on free speech. While the Court recognized that limits on sources (i.e., contributions) also involved curtailment of free speech, it held that *reasonable* limits could be justified by government's need to protect the system from real or apparent corruption arising from *quid pro quo* relationships between campaign donors and candidates. By equating the right to spend money with the right of free speech, and by differentiating between money given to a candidate and money spent by a candidate, this and subsequent lower court rulings have had a profound effect on the regulation and flow of money in U.S. politics.

Public Financing

Other democracies' far greater use of the public treasury in financing elections marks another way in which the U.S. political system is different. Government subsidies to parties are common in the international arena, and free broadcasting privileges are often facilitated by government ownership of major broadcast stations, unlike in the United States. The combined effect of direct subsidies and free broadcast time is reduced pressure on politicians to raise campaign money.

Some Americans have long favored similar government subsidies for election campaigns, as well as having free or reduced-rate broadcast time mandated of private sector broadcasters. And they have had some success in getting their ideas enacted. These policies, however, have met with resistance on philosophical grounds (that is, requiring taxpayers to support

candidates whom they may oppose) and on practical grounds (such as how to devise a completely fair system of subsidizing campaigns).

Those who support public funding for candidates succeeded in the 1970s in enacting such a system for presidential elections and for some state and local elections as well, but not for elections of members of the U.S. Congress. Since 1976, major-party presidential nominees have automatically qualified for a substantial general election subsidy (some $67 million each in 2000 for Republican George W. Bush and Democrat Al Gore). Parties receive subsidies for their nominating conventions, and, in primary elections, government funds are available to match small individual donations to candidates.

In exchange for receiving funding, candidates must agree to limits on campaign spending, which the Supreme Court permitted because of their voluntary nature. The effectiveness of these limits, however, has been eroded by the ability of interested individuals and groups to spend money to assist candidates in ways that are legal but are beyond the levels envisioned by federal law ("soft money," as discussed below).

Major Principles of Federal Law

Since the 1970s, three major principles have governed federal campaign finance law in the United States, applying to all elections for president and the Congress. (Each of the 50 states has its own rules for state and local elections.) These principles are as follows.

- Public Disclosure of Financial Activity

Public visibility of money in elections, facilitating scrutiny by opposing parties and candidates and by the media, is seen as the greatest deterrent to corruption that might arise from campaign contributions and expenditures. About this aspect of government regulation, there is largely a consensus, at least in principle. At the federal level, this involves periodic reports, with aggregate totals and detailed breakdowns for amounts above $200.

- Prohibitions on Sources of Funds

Corporations, national banks, and labor unions have long been prohibited from using funds from their treasuries—corporate profits and union-dues money—to influence federal elections (although many states allow such sources in their elections). These entities may, however, set up political action committees to raise voluntary donations from executives and stockholders and union members, respectively. These funds may be used in federal elections, thus bringing the sponsoring corporation's or union's influence to bear. Also prohibited in all *U.S. elections are campaign funds from foreign nationals.*

• Limitations on Sources of Funds

Federal law limits the amounts contributed to candidates, parties, and groups involved in federal elections, whether by individuals, PACs, or parties. An individual may give $2,000 to a candidate in an election and a total of $95,000 to all candidates, parties, and PACs in a two-year election cycle. A PAC can give $5,000 per election to a candidate, but there is no aggregate limit on all such contributions from a single entity.

Reform Efforts

The issues raised by money and politics have made campaign finance reform a perennial topic of debate in the United States. Throughout the 1980s and 1990s, reform advocates sought unsuccessfully to augment the regulatory regime enacted in the 1970s so as to reduce the role and importance of money in the political system.

The law that was finally passed in 2002, however, bore little resemblance to its precursors. Whereas these measures sought to *improve* the existing federal regulatory system, the goal of the Bipartisan Campaign Reform Act of 2002, or BCRA (familiarly known as McCain-Feingold for the two lead senators who sponsored the law), is to save that system, by bringing under federal regulation activities that proponents saw as circumventing federal campaign finance law.

The Rise of "Big" Money

Beginning in the 1980s, national political parties began to raise money in amounts far beyond what technically was permitted under federal law, although ostensibly not for use in federal elections per se. This return of the "fat cat"—the powerful, wealthy contributor presumably reined in under the 1970s reforms—heralded the rise of "soft money" in American elections. The term describes funds that are raised and spent outside the federal election regulatory framework but that may have at least an indirect impact on federal elections (in contrast to "hard money," which is raised and spent according to federal election law).

Typically, these soft-money donations, in amounts and from sources prohibited in federal elections, were distributed to affiliated state parties for use in grassroots operations and voter mobilization efforts. By bolstering such activities, they inevitably assisted federal candidates as well as the state and local races at which they purportedly were aimed. In addition, the concerted fund-raising efforts by national party officials and by federal candidates and officials suggested that these donations were sought primarily to assist federal candidates.

Only during the 1996 national elections, however, did the belief that the regulatory system was breaking down become pervasive. Not only was $900 million in soft money raised by the political parties that year, but interest groups and political parties discovered another way to influence federal elections outside of federal restrictions: election-related issue advocacy. This form of soft money involves communications that discuss candidates in conjunction with particular issue positions, but without explicitly urging the defeat or election of clearly identified candidates.

Because most lower courts have interpreted the *Buckley v. Valeo* ruling as requiring such explicit wording in order to subject communications to government regulation, groups could present public information that encouraged positive or negative views of public officials who also happened to be candidates in forthcoming elections, without being subject to federal election law restrictions. For 1996 and subsequent elections, it was estimated that tens of millions of dollars were spent in this manner, with accurate levels impossible to determine because little or no disclosure was required.

The Impact of McCain-Feingold

After 1996, reformers shifted their focus from limits on PACs and campaign spending and on public financing to closing loopholes they perceived as rendering federal regulation of money in politics increasingly meaningless. The McCain-Feingold law of 2002 generally bans national parties and federal candidates or officials from raising and spending soft money; likewise, it bans state and local parties from spending soft money on what are defined as "federal election activities." With regard to issue advocacy, the new law requires disclosure of all political advertisements referring to clearly identified federal candidates broadcast within 30 days of a primary or 60 days of a general election, and it prohibits sponsorship with union or corporate treasury funds.

Throughout the years of debate preceding passage of McCain-Feingold, the question of constitutionality hung over the discussions. This was perhaps inevitable given the experience of the 1976 *Buckley v. Valeo* ruling, which left in its wake a system not envisioned by Congress but with far-reaching implications for the flow of money in federal elections. The closer the legislation came to enactment, the more the question of constitutionality became the focus of the debate. With campaigning for the 2004 elections already under way and politicians seeking to adapt to the new law, the political community eagerly awaits the expedited judicial review mandated by McCain-Feingold.

McConnell v. FEC

On May 2, 2003, the first of these rulings came when the U.S. District Court for the District of Columbia, in *McConnell v. FEC*, struck down the blanket prohibition on soft-money raising by national parties and its use by state and local parties, but retained the bans on public communications that may more directly affect federal elections and on soft-money raising by federal candidates and officials. In addition, the court struck down the regulation of all broadcast ads referring to federal candidates, based on time period, but surprised observers by allowing regulation based on the more subjective standard of whether an advertisement supported or opposed a federal candidate, regardless of when it was disseminated. This ruling was later stayed, to minimize confusion for those already campaigning for the 2004 elections, pending a final decision by the Supreme Court. [The Court upheld the constitutionality of McCain-Feingold in December 2003.]

VIEWPOINT 3

> "[Election] advertising campaigns pushed the borders of federal law and directly challenged the ability of federal regulators to control presidential campaign spending."

Campaign Financing Takes Advantage of Legal Loopholes

Anthony Corrado

In the viewpoint that follows, Anthony Corrado examines campaign financing in the 2000 presidential election in order to highlight problems with the current system. Specifically, Corrado argues that federal regulators have a difficult time enforcing existing laws. One result of this is that some groups take advantage of loopholes in order to advance the candidate they support, even though many are aware that their efforts are unethical. Corrado is a professor of government at Colby College in Waterville, Maine, and the author of Campaign Finance Reform: Beyond the Basics.

As you read, consider the following questions:

1. What is the main federal law that regulates spending in presidential elections, as cited by Corrado?

Anthony Corrado, "Financing the 2000 Presidential General Election," *Financing the 2000 Election*, ed. David B. Magleby, Washington, DC: Brookings Institution Press, 2002. www.brookings.edu.

2. What are political action committees, and what function do they perform in presidential elections according to the author?
3. What stipulations must a candidate abide by in order to gain public funds for his or her campaign, as reported by Corrado?

The 2000 presidential general election was one of the closest contests in the nation's history. It was also one of the most expensive. Spurred by tight margins and a permissive regulatory environment, the candidates and their supporters took advantage of every available opportunity to raise and spend money in the hope that additional resources would provide the narrow margin of votes needed to win. When the race finally ended, after an extraordinary postelection recount contest in Florida and a historic Supreme Court decision that was determined by a five-to-four vote, more than $300 million had been spent in the general election alone. This sum included more than $100 million in expenditures that were made outside of the spending ceilings imposed on presidential candidates and party committees by federal law.

FECA

While most of the funding in the presidential contest came from sources regulated by the Federal Election Campaign Act (FECA), the steep rise in the amount of unregulated money, especially party soft money funding, characterized the financial activity in the race. As in 1996, the public monies available to the candidates were supplemented by substantial party money and significant issue advocacy and voter mobilization spending by interest groups. The Democratic and Republican national party committees aggressively solicited soft dollars on behalf of their respective presidential nominees and spent tens of millions of these dollars on activities designed to assist these candidates in their campaigns. A large share of these funds was spent on broadcast advertising, especially issue advocacy advertisements with messages crafted to support one candidate or the other. These ads, because they did not "expressly advocate" the election or defeat of a specific candidate, were exempt from the limits governing party expenditures made in coordination with a candidate and could be financed with combinations of hard and soft money. Organized groups mimicked these tactics, using their political funds, which in most cases were not subject to the FECA contribution restrictions, to sponsor issue ads of their own. Consequently, the public subsidies given to the candidates essentially served as a floor for campaign spending. The only ceiling on spending, for practical purposes, was the fund-raising capacity of parties and organized groups and their willingness to devote resources to the race at the top of the ticket.

Funding Strategies

The flow of money in the presidential contest reinforced the financial patterns established in 1996 and refined in the 1998 midterm elections. So the strategies employed were not new. But in 1996, the use of party issue ads to supplement the public monies available to presidential candidates was considered a bold innovation; four years later, it had become the standard approach. This change was largely a response to Federal Election Commission (FEC) regulatory decisions issued in the aftermath of the 1996 election, which failed to restrain the new model of finance that emerged in that contest and thus effectively sanctioned the efforts of party committees to circumvent the FECA limits. Parties therefore operated as if there were no limits at all on their funding. In fact, with respect to the sources of money and amounts spent, the party activity in 2000 was more akin to the financial activity in the 1972 election, the last election before the adoption of the FECA contribution limits, than to any election conducted under the regulatory framework put in place after the 1972 election. The parties freely engaged in raising contributions of unlimited amounts from individuals, political action committees (PACs), corporations, and labor unions. They also spent unlimited amounts, and for the first time since the enactment of the FECA, the parties spent more on television advertising in the presidential race than the candidates did themselves.

The role of the parties was the most prominent but only one of the notable aspects of the financing of the presidential campaign. The contest also featured the first dispute between candidates within a party over the entitlement to general election public funding. It included the first instance of recount financing in a presidential race. Most important, it evidenced the further development of a new model of presidential campaign finance that signaled, in effect, the collapse of the FECA regulatory structure....

The 2000 Elections

The regulations governing campaign funding and the strategic context of the race dictated the financing of the 2000 election. An increasingly lax regulatory structure gave candidates and their supporters ample opportunities to spend money on the presidential race, and the strategic context gave them the incentive to do so. Although the strategic factors ultimately determined the level of spending, the regulatory factors played the more important role in defining what types of financial activity paid for the campaign.

Under the FECA provisions, a major party presidential candidate who accepted public funding received a subsidy equal to the total amount of the general election expenditure ceiling, which was $67.6 million in 2000. A minor party candidate could receive a proportional share of this subsidy if the party received 5 percent or more of the vote in the previous election. A candidate who receives partial public funding is allowed to solicit private contributions to raise money to make up the balance between the amount received in public fund-

Top 15 PACs in 2004 Election (by Contributions)

1	MoveOn PAC	$30,043,750
2	Emily's List	$26,051,693
3	America Coming Together	$15,154,735
4	American Federation of State, County, & Municipal Employees	$14,056,945
5	UAW VCAP (UAW Voluntary Community Action Program)	$13,336,541
6	NRA Political Victory Fund	$12,772,488
7	Service Employees International Union Committee on Political Education (SEIU COPE)	$12,461,614
8	DRIVE (Democrat Republican Independent Voter Education)	$10,468,934
9	Republican Issues Campaign	$7,959,860
10	Voice of Teachers for Education/ Committee on Policy Education of New York State United Teachers (VOTE/ COPE OF NYSUT)	$7,634,014
11	National Association of Realtors	$7,349,116
12	1199 Service Employees International Union Political Action Fund	$6,739,856
13	CWA-COPE Political Contributions Committee	$6,486,348
14	Association of Trial Lawyers of America	$6,482,147
15	International Brotherhood of Electrical Workers Committee on Political Education	$6,317,770

U.S. Federal Election Commission, April 13, 2005.

ing and the overall expenditure ceiling. Any private monies raised for this purpose must come from contributions of no more than $1,000 per individual or $5,000 per PAC [political action committee].

To receive public funding, a candidate must agree to abide by the spending limit and refrain from soliciting additional private contributions. A candidate may, however, raise additional funds in amounts no greater than $1,000 from individuals to finance the legal and accounting costs incurred to comply with the law. These General Election Legal and Accounting Compliance funds (GELAC) are exempt from the spending ceiling. In addition, the Democratic and Republican national party committees are each allowed to spend a limited amount in coordination with, or on behalf of, their respective nominees. In 2000, the limit on such coordinated spending was $13.7 million for each party. All of the monies used for coordinated expenditures must come from donations raised under federal contribution limits.

A Model Election for Reform Needs

In recent elections, the FECA's relatively simple scheme for financing presidential campaigns has been replaced by increasingly complicated and sophisticated financial schemes that revolve around the parties' continuing efforts to exploit their ability to spend soft money in ways that benefit a presidential candidate. The most recent major innovation emerged in 1996, when first the Democratic Party and then the Republican Party supplemented the finances of their presidential nominees by spending millions of dollars on issue advertisements that featured President Bill Clinton and his opponent, Robert Dole. The parties claimed that these advertisements were not campaign expenditures subject to FECA restrictions because they did not use the "magic words," such as "vote for" or "vote against," which most previous court decisions had deemed necessary for the application of federal limits. The committees therefore paid for the advertising with a mixture of hard and soft money, mostly soft money, eventually spending a combined total of more than $65 million, not including the coordinated expenditures they were allowed to make under the law.

These advertising campaigns pushed the borders of federal law and directly challenged the ability of federal regulators to control presidential campaign spending. If such actions were allowable, then the regulations were basically meaningless, since candidates could rely on party monies or other outside funding to assist their campaigns, regardless of any spending limits. Moreover, party committees could work with candidates to raise soft money that could be used to finance activities designed to benefit their campaigns. But whether such efforts were permissible under the FECA provisions was uncertain in 1996. While party lawyers claimed that these methods of subverting the rules were legal, they were based on gray areas in the law that needed further definition and regulatory interpretation.

Before the 2000 elections, the Federal Election Commission (FEC) took no action to prohibit or even deter the financial schemes used in 1996. In conducting the required audit of the 1996 presidential campaigns, the FEC Audit Division determined that the party ads should be considered campaign expenses and recommended that the Clinton and Dole campaigns be penalized for exceeding spending limits and receiving "excessive contributions" from the party committees. But the commission voted 6 to 0 against the recommendation that the Clinton and Dole campaigns repay a total of $25 million to the federal treasury because they improperly benefited from party ads. The agency's Office of General Counsel also recommended an enforcement proceeding, based on its conclusion that the Democratic Party's ads were coordinated with the Clinton campaign and therefore constituted illegal soft money expenditures and campaign contributions. The FEC, however, did not accept these recommendations. Instead, the commission deadlocked on a vote of 3 to 3 on the recommendations, and the investigation was closed. In making this decision, the FEC did not set forth a position on whether soft money funded issue ads that featured a federal candidate or were coordinated with a candidate were permissible under the law. The FEC simply left the law in limbo, though in a lighter shade of gray, since with respect to future election activity, no decision was a decision.

FEC Investigations

The FEC also investigated the 1996 political activities of the AFL-CIO, one of the nation's largest labor unions. This enforcement case centered on the assistance that the AFL-CIO provided to Democratic candidates during the 1996 campaign. At issue was whether the union had improperly coordinated its activities with the Democrats and thus made improper contributions to the party and its candidates. The investigation, which produced 35,000 pages of documents, found that "national and state committees of the Democratic Party provided the AFL-CIO or its state affiliates nearly total access to their plans, projects, activities, and needs, at least with respect to a major voter mobilization program in each state known as the 'Coordinated Campaign.'" The contact between the union and the Democrats included the labor federation's ability to "approve or disapprove" party political plans, but because the evidence did not show that the union had engaged in communications with the general public, as opposed to its own members, the FEC voted to dismiss the case. In other words, it did not attempt to enforce its own coordination rules and instead deferred to recent judicial interpretations that have provided independent groups with wide latitude to consult with parties and candidates in formulating their own plans without violating campaign finance laws.

Congress and the Department of Justice also investigated the financial activities associated with the 1996 presidential campaign, but neither took actions that would prevent similar efforts in the future. The FEC considered making new rules on soft money coordination, but discussions in both 1998 and 2000 failed to produce any new guidelines or restrictions.

Thus, despite the major controversy sparked by soft money contributions in the 1996 election, no changes were made in the regulatory structure to stem the use of soft money before the start of the 2000 campaign. Instead, federal regulators essentially gave candidates and parties a green light to continue relying on soft money to subvert the contribution and spending limits.

Minor Campaign Finance Reforms

The FEC did make some minor changes in their regulations to try to address one of the factors that stimulated the move to issue advertising: the problem of financing campaign activities during the period between the effective end of the presidential selection process and the national nominating conventions. Because of the increasingly compressed front-loading of the presidential primary calendar, the party nominations are being decided earlier and earlier in the process. In 1996 the battle for nomination in both parties was over by the end of March, which left the prospective victors, President Bill Clinton and Republican challenger Robert Dole, with a period of about four months to continue campaigning before the national conventions. But the spending limits imposed on prenomination campaigns, which were established more than twenty years ago, are not designed to accommodate the front-loaded primary process, especially in the case of a hotly contested contest. So Dole had already essentially reached the spending limit by the end of March. As a result, he was no longer able to spend monies to continue aggressive campaigning, even though two months remained before the official end of the state primaries in the first week of June. Clinton, however, had $20 million left to spend, largely because he was unopposed and had been the beneficiary of $34 million in Democratic Party issue advertising that promoted his reelection. The Republican Party therefore financed issue ads supporting Dole to provide his campaign with a form of "bridge financing" to help him compete until the general election public funding was issued at thc time of the convention.

VIEWPOINT 4

"The presidential public funding system is a remarkable example of minority rule."

Public Financing of Presidential Elections Is a Waste of Taxpayer Money

John Samples

Public financing of presidential elections was put in place to increase voter participation and to free candidates from having to devote the majority of their time to fund-raising. In this viewpoint, John Samples contends that the system has failed to achieve these goals and instead benefits mainly a small minority of wealthy elites. Samples is the director of the Center for Responsible Government at the libertarian Cato Institute and the author of the Fallacy of Campaign Finance Reform.

As you read, consider the following questions:

1. Has the system of public financing made it easier or more difficult for third-party candidates to campaign for the presidency, according to Samples?

John Samples, "The Failures of Taxpayer Financing of Presidential Campaigns," *Policy Analysis*, vol. 500, November 25, 2003, pp. 7–14. www.cato.org.

2. Has public financing increased or decreased the number of candidates in presidential primaries, in the author's opinion?
3. Has voter participation improved as a result of public financing, in Samples's opinion?

We would expect that the availability of public money would increase the absolute number of candidates for the presidency compared with elections prior to 1976. By subsidizing the cost of running for president, taxpayer financing makes it easier to mount a campaign. Has public financing led to more candidates for the presidency?

We can set aside the major party candidates in the general elections for the presidency. They have all taken taxpayer financing. However, prior to 1976, the two parties found the means to finance the campaigns of their candidates. In that sense, the presidential funding system did not change whether the major parties had a presidential candidate. No doubt the system did make it easier for the parties and their candidates to raise the money necessary for campaigns. But making life easier for major party presidential candidates was not a goal of taxpayer financing.

Third Parties

Apart from the major party candidates, nine presidential candidates in the general elections since 1948 have received more than 1 percent of the total vote in an election. Five of those candidates ran after the presidential public funding system was created in 1976. Not all five accepted public financing. Ross Perot did not accept taxpayer financing in 1992, preferring to spend $65 million of his own money on his candidacy. Ed Clark, the Libertarian candidate in 1980, also did not take taxpayer financing. In all, six of the nine non-major-party candidates who made a mark in presidential elections after 1948 ran their campaigns without the help of the taxpayer.

Moreover, the two top vote getters during the period—George Wallace in 1968 and Ross Perot in 1992—brought their campaigns before the electorate without subsidies. Public presidential funding might be credited with three additional presidential campaigns in seven general elections (Ralph Nader in 2000, Ross Perot in 1996, and John Anderson in 1980). The private system in place prior to 1976 produced four serious candidates apart from the major party candidates in the previous seven general elections. In other words, the taxpayer has spent $153 million to support general election campaigns, an investment that has yielded one candidate less than the private system of financing it replaced.

Candidates in Primaries

What about the party nominations? Surely the availability of taxpayer money has increased the number of candidates contending for each major party's nomination. Most of the money paid out by the presidential public funding system has gone to fund the conventions of the two major political parties (10 percent of all funding) and their candidates in the general election (61 percent of all funding). Candidates running in the primaries have received a little more than $506 million, or about 29 percent of all outlays by the system. That money has funded 83 candidates in the primaries. Of those, 71 were candidates for the nominations of the two major political parties. Of those 71 candidates, 55 received more than 1 percent of the total number of votes cast in a party's presidential primaries for a given year, an average of 7.8 candidates each presidential election....

Primaries

For purposes of argument, we might ignore the data on primary candidates from the party-centric era and look only at the years when primaries dominated the selection of presidential nominees. Indeed, the importance of the primary might itself be an incentive for candidates to enter the race. How can we tell whether the primary or public funding had a greater effect on the number of primary candidates? In 1972 party primaries had a strong influence on the nomination of each party's candidate for the presidency. Democratic primary voters directly selected 66.5 percent of the delegates to their presidential nominating convention; Republican primary voters picked 58.2 percent of the delegates. The presidential funding system did not yet exist. The 1972 election should indicate the influence of the incentives connected to primaries (apart from the money provided by public financing) on the number of primary candidates for the presidency.

In 1972 a total of 12 primary candidates got more than 1 percent of the overall vote in the respective party primaries. That total equals the number in 1976 and is greater than the number in all subsequent years. In fact, the number of primary candidates is almost double the post-1976 average. The data suggest that introducing public financing might have led to a decline in the number of primary candidates after 1976....

A final point: Many more primary candidates received public funding (75) after 1976 than received more than 1 percent of the their party's vote (55). The number of funded candidates after 1976 equals the number of candidates getting more than 1 percent of the vote prior to 1976 (75 candidates). The marginal effect of taxpayer financing seems to have been to subsidize abject failure (or an ego trip) for 20 candidates. What the system has not done is produce more presidential primary candidates than the older system it replaced. From the taxpayer's point of view, that result hardly seems worth $500 million.

Greens and the Reform Party

The two major political parties have dominated general elections for president for more than a century. The presidential public funding system has done little to promote competition to the two-party system. The Greens and the Reform Party must be counted as the only two third parties with sizable followings to receive funding from the taxpayer. Ross Perot, the publicly funded Reform candidate in the general election of 1996, received a little more than 8 percent of the total vote. By 2000 the Reform Party candidate, Patrick Buchanan, received less than half of 1 percent of the popular vote despite spending more than $13 million in public funding on the effort. Ralph Nader, the Green Party candidate in 2000, received 2.7 percent of the national vote. The availability of taxpayer financing has not enabled any new parties to challenge the two-party duopoly in presidential elections. To the contrary, the presidential public funding system has subsidized the two major parties and their general election candidates to the tune of $1.27 billion.

Finally, the taxpayer has also funded a few fringe candidates over the years. Lyndon LaRouche, a perennial candidate in Democratic presidential primaries, initially ran for president in 1976 and has been a candidate in every election since, including a 1992 effort from prison. He was serving 5 years of a 15-year sentence for mail fraud and defaulting on more than $30 million in loans from campaign supporters. LaRouche recently denounced "leading members of the Synarchist banking crowd, which ... is currently involved in a criminal conspiracy to bring down the world financial system, in what might be called a 'Financial 9-11,' and use the collapse to impose a dictatorship." LaRouche has received more than $5.5 million from the public to underwrite his five attempts at gaining the Democratic nomination for the presidency. Lenora Fulani of the New Alliance Party once headed a political group deemed "armed and dangerous" by the Federal Bureau of Investigation. She received almost $4 million in her two runs for the presidency. John Hagelin, the head of the Natural Law Party, might thank the taxpayer for the $1.75 million he has obtained from the presidential public funding system. Hagelin foresees an ideal government that combines "modern science and ancient Vedic Science." Hagelin proposed in 1999 to end violence in Kosovo by sending there an elite group of "Yogic flyers," who would levitate themselves through meditation thereby spreading peace "with a quantum-mechanical consciousness field." Whether propagating the views of LaRouche, Fulani, and Hagelin at a cost of more than $11 million to the taxpayer improved American democracy might be debated in the abstract. It is fair to say that average Americans would be enraged to learn that they are subsidizing such efforts.

Compared with the system it replaced, the presidential public funding system has failed to generate more public discussion or competition by increasing the number of general election candidates, primary election candidates, or challenges to the two-party system. The average citizen might be tempted to think that almost $2 billion in subsidies should have more to show in fostering presidential candidates and electoral competition. As far as candidates go, much of what has happened in presidential elections since 1976 would have happened anyway. The two parties would have funded their presidential candidates, as many or perhaps more primary contenders would have run, party conventions would have been funded, and Ross Perot would have run in 1992. Public financing has not so much changed what happens as who pays for what happens. Taxpayers will win no prizes for guessing who that might be.

Public Participation

The presidential public funding system also aimed at increasing public participation in elections by allowing individuals to easily give a small contribution to presidential campaigns by checking a box on their federal income tax form. One might assume that taxpayer financing would easily foster more participation through contributions. After all, taxpayers need only check a box on their tax form, and their contribution to the

Democrats Are Most Likely to Accept Public Funds

One criticism leveled against public financing is that Democrats use—and are therefore advantaged by—programs more than Republicans and other political parties. In the 2004 Maine general election, for instance, Democrats were more likely than any other party to accept public funds: 86 percent of all Democratic legislative candidates participated in the public financing program. This rate outpaced Green Party candidates (73 percent), Republican candidates (70 percent) and Independents (67 percent). In fact, Democrats made up 50 percent of the candidates who accepted public funds, even though there were more Republicans than Democrats on the ballot. Similarly, Democrats were more likely than Republicans and third party candidates to participate in Arizona's public financing program in each of its past three elections. In 2004, 70 percent of Democrats accepted public funds, compared to 59 percent of Republicans and 13 percent of Libertarians. Democratic participation in New York City's public financing program has also far outpaced that of Republican candidates.

Steven M. Levin, Keeping It Clean: Public Financing in American Elections, *2006.*

presidential fund does not increase their tax burden. Here again experience contravenes that expectation.

The participation rate in the presidential public funding system has declined steadily since its inception. The highest participation rate came in the early years of the fund when as many as 28 percent of taxpayers diverted money to the system. Recently, the rate has been slightly higher than 10 percent. Survey research indicates that in 2000 about 12 percent of Americans over the age of 18 gave to political candidates, party committees, or political organizations. Compared with the private system, public financing does not broaden participation in donating to campaigns.

Moreover, participation in the presidential public funding system continues to steadily fall. If the current trend continues (and it has already continued for about 20 years), the system will have a participation rate of 5 percent by 2008.

In Defense of the System

Defenders of taxpayer financing have often argued (and argue still) that, if the checkoff had more publicity, it would attract higher participation. As far back as 1989, the Federal Election Commission [FEC] became concerned about falling participation rates and supported publicity campaigns in 1991 and 1992 to inform citizens about the program. The FEC claims those campaigns reached 90 million Americans in 1991 and 203 million in 1992. Those efforts had little effect. The FEC's efforts began in March 1991. In April 1991 the participation rate for the program was 19.5 percent. In 1992, after a year of publicity, the participation rate *fell* to 17.7 percent, a 12 percent decline! In 1993, after a year of even more publicity, the participation rate rose to 18.9 percent, which was higher than that in 1992 but still below the starting point of the publicity campaign in 1991. In other words, the FEC did what the defenders of the system wanted and publicized the program. Those efforts resulted in the participation rate declining further. In 1994 the rate dropped again (to 14.5 percent), which meant it had declined 25 percent in three years, the period of steepest decline in participation in the history of the program.

Some people now argue for additional efforts to persuade taxpayers to check off their returns in support of public financing. Such an effort would be no more likely to succeed than the earlier one in the 1990s. Apparently, the more Americans learned about the presidential public funding system, the less inclined they were to check the box on their tax form.

Why should taxpayers be taxed to support a publicity campaign for a program they have already rejected?

Lack of Participation

The lack of participation is not an aberration caused by the public's lack of knowledge of the presidential program. The public's rejection of public financing is not limited to federal schemes. The 13 states that had checkoff schemes for taxpayer financing saw a steady decline in participation from 1975 to 1994. The typical checkoff program dropped from 20 percent participation to 11 percent during that period....

Such public opposition to public financing bears on current policy debates. Two members of the FEC as well as a separate task force have proposed increasing both spending by the presidential fund and the amount of the checkoff. They propose to spend more on campaigns through public financing, even though Americans suspect that such programs "would cost taxpayers too much money." The FEC commissioners are concerned about a funding shortfall in 2008. Yet this continual crisis of the presidential financing system comes directly from its lack of popular support. If even as few as 20 percent of Americans supported the current checkoff, funding would not be a problem. Supporters of the system say inflation has eaten away at the value of the checkoff. If the original checkoff sum of $1 had kept up with inflation, it would have been worth $3.22 in 2002. That would improve the system's finances slightly, but it would hardly make much difference at current participation rates. Some people now urge the checkoff sum be increased to $5, a real increase of 50 percent. Supporters of the system are trying to obscure its central failing: it lacks popular support. A lack of democratic legitimacy cannot be set right by technical fixes or by extracting ever more wealth from taxpayers.

The presidential public funding system is a remarkable example of minority rule. It allows about 10 percent of taxpayers to spend taxes paid by everyone on presidential campaigns by the major political parties. If the system did not exist, its funding could be returned to current or future taxpayers. In other words, the presidential public funding system allows a small percentage of taxpayers (10 percent and dropping) to tax either the other 90 percent of current taxpayers or all future taxpayers. The system allows a small number of citizens with strong antipathy to private funding of presidential campaigns to compel the overwhelming majority to pay the costs associated with their antipathy. That can hardly be democratic or efficient.

Michael Toner, a commissioner on the FEC, summarized the democracy deficit of the presidential fund:

> Any system of public financing must have popular support to succeed. Today's low taxpayer checkoff rates cast serious doubt on whether the public financing system has this support.... When only one in nine taxpayers are [*sic*] participating, it is very difficult to conclude that the public financing system has broad popular support.

Why continue at taxpayer expense a program that reflects nothing more than the preferences of a small minority?

Fund-raising Problems

In *Buckley v. Valeo* the Supreme Court said the government had a vital interest "in relieving major-party candidates from the rigors of soliciting private contributions." No doubt fund-raising is a problem for candidates. Many of them have testified that they do not enjoy the task. But that is a private burden and a private problem. Why are the rigors of fundraising a public problem that justifies public subsidies?

We might pause to reflect on the asymmetry here. Americans have to work to make a living and to pay the taxes that support the government. In contrast, taxpayer financing assumes that candidates for office cannot be expected to work to fully fund their campaigns for office. Public financing thus offers "welfare for politicians" funded by Americans who work for a living and consumed by politicians who are not willing to support themselves. That difference may go a way toward explaining public antipathy to public financing in general and the apathy toward the presidential system in particular.

Of course, defenders of the program see things differently. They argue that Congress might have assumed that candidates for the presidency would better use their time on some task other than raising campaign funds....

The Costs of Fund-raising

Moreover, critics say, absent public funding, the costs of fund-raising would be astronomical. Without the system, a leading defender of pubic financing argues, "presidential candidates would have to devote most of their time to the burdensome task of raising money," especially for general elections. Writing in 1993, [scholar] Anthony Corrado speculated that, absent taxpayer financing, presidential candidates would rely more on PAC [political action committee] donations and soft money to fund their campaigns.

In economic life, government regulations often lead to problems that prompt calls for more regulation. So it is with the rigors of fundraising. Under current law, candidates must raise money within specific and aggregate contribution limits. Until 2002 the limit for individuals was $1,000. Compared with a system of higher or no limits, the current system inevitably requires more time and resources to raise the funds necessary to run for office. The costs (including the candidate's time) of finding and persuading a donor are fixed while the returns from that investment are limited. If the returns were higher or unlimited, the "rigors" of raising necessary funding (including the candidate's time and effort) would be lower.

Federal election law itself (though not public financing per se) causes much of the problem the presidential system purports to solve.

Absent taxpayer financing, would presidential candidates have to spend "most of their time" raising money? During the primary contests of 2000, George W. Bush declined public funding. His primary and general election campaigns spent more than $100 million, a sum entirely adequate to his task. Bush did not spend all his time fundraising. Throughout his public and private career, President Bush has delegated tasks with clear goals and constraints. Bush and his team put together an organization of fundraisers called "Pioneers," each of whom pledged to raise $100,000 for the Bush campaign. Doing that within the contribution limits set by federal law required the organization to develop an extensive network of contributors and fundraisers. In other words, the candidate had to build a fundraising organization by recruiting talented individuals with fresh ideas about fundraising who in turn brought in other fundraisers and contributors. Bush had more than enough money for the primaries, and we have no evidence that the candidate felt pressured by his oversight of, and contribution to, fundraising.

The Benefits of Fund-raising

Indeed, the fundraising challenge, though partially created by perverse regulations, serves the public by providing valuable information about a presidential candidate. Presidents must persuade people to do their will and organize an effective executive branch. Meeting the fundraising challenge (or failing to do so) tells Americans a lot about a candidate's ability to persuade others, to organize an undertaking, and to exert leadership. Moreover, fundraising shows that the candidate has persuaded some individuals to actually spend money supporting his campaign. Such support is far more serious and real than the backing revealed in a public opinion poll. The fundraising challenge is so large that a candidate cannot do it by himself. He has to persuade talented individuals to join his campaign and to help him raise money. They in turn must create and administer an organization that meets the candidate's goals. Far from being a waste of time, the rigors of fundraising are a good test for anyone who wants to be president, and the public benefits by knowing that a candidate can meet that challenge. Given the relevance of fundraising to presidential performance, the time spent by candidates on that task is well worth less time spent with voters or on enhancing the advantages of incumbency.

The Superiority of Private Financing

By making it easier to run for the highest office, the presidential funding system deprives the electorate of important information about a candidate. Absent the system, would a candidate have evinced the persuasiveness and organizational ability to meet the fundraising challenge? The voters will never know because the taxpayer provided much of the candidate's funding.

Measured by its own standards, the presidential campaign finance system has come a cropper. It has not led to more candidates or electoral competition or new parties vying for the presidency. Most important, the American taxpayer has rejected the system as fewer and fewer citizens check off the tax form to contribute to the system. By the election of 2008, the system may be supported by half as many Americans as make private campaign contributions. The system lacks democratic legitimacy, a failure that cannot be overcome by adjusting this or that technical requirement. Why should a system without any popular support impose costs on current and future taxpayers?

VIEWPOINT 5

> *"Fundraising should not be the only, or even the central, requirement for a presidential nomination."*

Public Election Financing Should Be Expanded

Norman J. Ornstein

The 2004 presidential election was the most expensive in history. In the following viewpoint Norman J. Ornstein argues that one way to limit campaign spending by individual candidates is to increase public financing in order to remove pressures on candidates to raise more money. The author contends that increased public financing will produce better candidates and free potential presidents from spending too much time on fund-raising. Ornstein is a resident scholar at the American Enterprise Institute and the author of a number of books on American politics.

As you read, consider the following questions:

1. How successful were George W. Bush and John F. Kerry in raising money in the 2004 presidential election, according to the author?

Norman J. Ornstein, "Presidential Campaign Financing Is Broken, but We Can Fix It," *Roll Call*, December 7, 2005. Reprinted with permission from *Roll Call*, December 7, 2005.

2. According to Ornstein, what are the main dangers of increased campaign spending in presidential elections?
3. What are the chances that campaign finance reform will be enacted, in the author's opinion?

The jockeying for position in both parties for the 2008 presidential race is already hot—maybe even hotter because of President Bush's travails....

Wherever I go, the second question, after the war in Iraq, is, "How would you handicap the White House pretenders/contenders?" There is something about human nature that has people as curious about the race ahead as the world today.

In my response, I give audiences a giant caveat: This time, keep in mind that the presidential campaign financing system is broken. Money will be even more crucial to the survival or feasibility of candidates than ever. Any handicapping has to take into account that if changes to the system aren't made, no viable candidate will be able to buy into it—that is, to take the bargain of receiving matching funds for contributions up to $250 in return for spending limits in each state and overall.

Actually, I think it's increasingly likely that in 2008, for the first time, the two parties' presidential candidates will forgo the huge public grant for the general election campaign and go it on their own.

Why? Because the system, established in 1976 after the Supreme Court's *Buckley v. Valeo* decision, has not adjusted the amounts for inflation since.

Just look at the numbers. A candidate who accepts the limits in 2008 will have to agree to an overall spending limit for the entire nominating season—right up to the party convention—of about $45 million.

Perhaps no candidate will have the success that President Bush and Sen. John Kerry (D-Mass.) had in 2004. Opting out of the system, they raised about $270 million and $235 mil-

The Benefits of Public Election Financing

Fair Elections—systems with full public financing of elections—would help improve the openness, honesty, and accountability of government. They would also free public officials to respond to the interests of voters without worrying about hurting their ability to raise money from deep-pocketed donors.

Most observers would agree that money plays far too large a role in elections—and that politicians spend too much time fundraising, detracting from the time they spend developing good public policy.

Common Cause, "Breaking Free with Fair Elections," 2007.

lion, respectively, in contributions of $2,000 or less. But, with individual contribution limits now up to $2,300 due to indexing for inflation, some candidates clearly come close. And even if they are not that close, they will have enough to fully swamp the poor schnooks who labor under a $45 million ceiling, not to mention the draconian limits in each state.

"So what?" is the question many observers might ask. The conservative Republicans who tried to zero out the presidential funding system entirely in [2005's] budget battles didn't get that far—they just saw an opening and an excuse to kill a long-standing reform for which they had a visceral distaste. But those who would ask the question deserve an answer.

It starts with this: A nonfunctioning system will give inordinate advantage to independently wealthy individuals, ideologues, or demagogues who can tap into a reservoir of funds from those who share intensely held views, and perhaps frontrunners who can stockpile funds early, leaving no room for a lesser-known candidate who excites voter interest by his or her campaigning in early state contests.

I don't have anything against money in politics. The fact is, it costs a lot to run a reasonable presidential campaign. But fundraising should not be the only, or even the central, requirement for a presidential nomination. And it should not be so important that it dominates every other candidate activity. Even now, at this ridiculously early stage, we can see the distortions in the process....

Interestingly, this time both parties have a problem with a broken system, and for the Republicans, the situation may even be worse.

In 2008 there will be no George W. Bush, who began in 2000 with such broad yearning for a viable GOP nominee that people were lining up to give him the maximum individual contribution (then $1,000) or who had the advantage of incumbency in 2004. If there is someone whose scenario comes close to his this time around, it is [Hillary] Clinton. But Clinton (and [John] McCain) notwithstanding, every other potential candidate in both parties would be better served if a viable alternative funding option existed. And McCain, as usual, is supporting reform even if it would not work to his advantage.

Some time ago, the savvy former GOP campaign lawyer Michael Toner, who now sits on the Federal Election Commission, grasped the problem and stepped up to the plate along with fellow Commissioner Scott Thomas, a Democrat. They came up with a constructive, reasonable and pragmatic restoration plan, to sharply raise the primary spending limit overall and state by state, to double the match from $250 to $500 and to index everything for inflation. They would make other positive changes, including raising the threshold a candidate must meet to qualify for matching funds, making them available earlier in the process and raising sharply the check-off amount on tax returns used to finance the system (and indexing that to inflation, too).

The case for doing this is strong—but at this point, the prognosis for action is dim. The party leaders have not focused on this at all. Legislation on campaign finance reform, whatever the substance, is anathema to many Republicans. There is no leadership from the White House. And in any event, the policy process in Congress is so dysfunctional that creating a climate for doing anything, much less gaining momentum, is difficult to imagine....

VIEWPOINT 6

> *"Today we are seeing the most systematic effort to censor and repress political speech ... since the ... 18th century."*

Limits on Contributions to Candidates Undermine Democracy

Newt Gingrich

In the following viewpoint Newt Gingrich argues that current efforts to reform campaign finance laws are a form of censorship. He uses historical examples, including the Alien and Sedition Act of 1798, combined with modern instances to illustrate his contention that all forms of speech, including monetary contributions, are vital to democracies. Newt Gingrich was formerly the Speaker of the House of Representatives and is the author of Rediscovering God in America: Reflections on the Role of Faith in our Nation's History and Future.

As you read, consider the following questions:

1. What historical act does the author compare to the McCain-Feingold law?
2. What are free speech "black-out" periods, according to Gingrich?

Newt Gingrich, "Blacking Out Speech," *National Review Online*, June 1, 2006. http://article.nationalreview.com.

3. Why, according to the author, should McCain-Feingold be repealed?

In the election of 1800, Thomas Jefferson became president and swept his party into power due, in part, to the country's overwhelming opposition to the Sedition Act of 1798. This act was a deliberate attempt by the Federalists in power to silence their political opponents.

The McCain-Feingold campaign-finance law enacted in 2002 is an equally dangerous modern-day assault on the First Amendment. It could more accurately be called the McCain-Feingold censorship law because it stifles political speech, protects incumbent politicians and consolidates power in Washington. This law is of the Congress, by the Congress, and for the Congress, because it protects members of Congress by silencing opposing points of view.

McCain-Feingold explicitly rejects James Madison's warning in Federalist [Paper] 10 that the destruction of liberty in pursuit of "curing the mischief of factions" is worse than the disease itself.

Madison and Thomas Jefferson were very sensitive to limitations on free speech because they lived through the Federalist efforts to criminalize political speech that was critical of the government. In response to the Sedition Act, Madison helped author the Virginia legislature's resolution that declared the act unconstitutional and stated that the law "ought to produce universal alarm, because it is leveled against that right of freely examining public characters and measures, and of free communication among the people thereon, which has ever been justly deemed, the only effectual guardian of every other right."

Jefferson helped write Kentucky's resolution, which called the Sedition Act a momentous regulation that wounds "the best rights of the citizen" and stated that "it would consider a silent acquiescence [to it] as highly criminal."

The Kentucky Resolutions

The representatives of the good people of this commonwealth in general assembly convened, having maturely considered the answers of sundry states in the Union, to their resolutions passed at the last session, respecting certain unconstitutional laws of Congress, commonly called the alien and sedition laws would be faithless indeed to themselves, and to those they represent, were they silently to acquiesce in principles and doctrines attempted to be maintained in all those answers, that of Virginia only excepted. To again enter the field of argument, and attempt more fully or forcibly to expose the unconstitutionality of those obnoxious laws, would, it is apprehended be as unnecessary as unavailing.

Kentucky General Assembly, 1799.

Modern Censorship

Today we are seeing the most systematic effort to censor and repress political speech by those in power since the Federalist overreach of the 18th century.

This is no exaggeration. The ongoing litigation between Wisconsin Right to Life (WRTL) and the Federal Election Commission (FEC) is a clear example of this.

WRTL attempted to air several issue ads in Wisconsin in the summer of 2004 calling on citizens to urge both of Wisconsin's U.S. Senators to oppose the filibustering of federal judicial appointments. McCain-Feingold, however, which Wisconsin Senator [Russ] Feingold cosponsored, contains a free speech "blackout period" before elections in which radio and television ads mentioning a candidate are deemed "electioneering communications" and are thus illegal. Therefore, since Senator Feingold was up for reelection in 60 days, this Wisconsin grassroots organization could not exercise their First Amendment rights and hold their elected representative accountable.

In Maine, we are now seeing the same thing happen again. The Christian Civic League of Maine (CCL) wants to broadcast a grassroots lobbying advertisement calling on Maine's senators—by name—to support the federal Marriage Protection Amendment before the Senate votes on it. The FEC objected and argued in federal district court that the Maine Christian Civic League can't use the Senators' names in the ad because it would fall within the McCain-Feingold free speech blackout period before Maine's [2006] primary election. The FEC won and this case is now on appeal to the Supreme Court, although with each passing day CCL is prohibited from running its grassroots advocacy ad.

Free Speech

This is horribly wrong. What would the Founding Fathers have thought of such free speech "blackout periods"? The days leading up to an election ought to be filled with debate. Free speech and activism, by informing and organizing the public, empower average citizens to promote a cause they believe in and to demand honest and responsive representation. Instead, the incumbent politicians that supported McCain-Feingold prefer to keep us quiet and prevent us from making noise about their records as Election Day gets closer.

A great travesty of the law is that it makes it harder for candidates of middle-class means to run for office at all. Instead, we have the example of how one candidate spent $100 million personally to buy a Senate seat, then a governorship, but while in the Senate voted for McCain-Feingold to limit every middle-class citizen to $2,500 in donations per election campaign. These rules move us dangerously closer to a plutocracy where the highest bidder can buy a seat.

In 1994, the Contract with America was a commitment to restore the bond of trust between individuals and their elected officials, putting the interests of the American people above all else. By limiting the ability of individuals or a collective group of individuals to participate and voice their opinion Congress is breaking this bond.

Repeal McCain-Feingold

We must repeal McCain-Feingold as the necessary first step towards reaffirming a bond of trust between the American people and their elected representatives.

A truly functioning campaign system would take power out of Washington and return it to its owners—the American people. Such a system would allow individuals to make unlimited contributions to candidates for Congress in their district, so long as it is reported immediately on the Internet and is transparent and accessible.

Once the American people come to understand the nature of McCain-Feingold's assault on liberty, there is no doubt that the final outcome will be the same today as it was for the Sedition Act: repeal. Those skeptical of seeking this reform should consider the words of Ronald Reagan: "If you're afraid of the future, then get out of the way, stand aside. The people of this country are ready to move again."

Periodical Bibliography

The following articles have been selected to supplement the diverse views presented in this chapter.

Perry Bacon Jr.	"The First Test: Who Can Raise the Most Cash," *Time*, February 5, 2007.
William F. Buckley Jr.	"Politics for a Billion," *National Review*, March 5, 2007.
Paul Bunner	"The Money Game," *Maclean's*, November 21, 2005.
John Cochran	"Public Financing: Rebirth or Irrelevance?" *CQ Weekly*, March 19, 2007.
Richard S. Dunham	"As Power Shifts, So Do the Dollars," *Business-Week*, April 23, 2007.
Joe Hadfield	"More than Survive, Parties Thrive Under New Campaign Finance Rules," *Campaigns & Elections*, April 2005.
P. J. O'Rourke	"Incumbent-Protection Acts," *Atlantic Monthly*, April 2005.
Edward T. Pound, Jennifer L. Jack, and Monica M. Ekman	"Straight Talk and Cold Cash," *U.S. News & World Report*, May 28, 2007.
David Weigal	"More Money, No Problem," *Reason*, May 2007.
Mark Wegner	"Report Offers Glimpse at Fundraising on Eve of Primaries," *CongressDaily*, May 26, 2006.

OPPOSING VIEWPOINTS® SERIES

Chapter 3

Do the Media Unfairly Influence Presidential Campaigns?

Chapter Preface

The media have become an integral part of the presidential election process. Politicians use newspapers, radio, the Internet, and television to communicate their messages to the American people. Candidates often stage media events, such as speeches or appearances at public venues, in an effort to attract the attention of journalists and reporters. In return, press coverage of candidates can shape opinions and either help or hurt campaigns. In fact, many candidates routinely blame the media for their failure to win primaries or elections. In some cases the media clearly are responsible for a candidate's loss. In 1984, Democrat Gary Hart challenged the media to find any fault with his behavior and famously declared, "Follow me around. I don't care. I'm serious. If anybody wants to put a tail on me, go ahead." Reporters did just that and discovered the senator was having an affair with a young model, Donna Rice. The story forced Hart to drop out of the race for the Democratic presidential nomination. Since the 1950s, presidential debates have been televised and sometimes these events can have a major impact on an election. For instance, in the 1960 election, many scholars argue that Richard M. Nixon's poor performance in his televised debate with John F. Kennedy cost him the election. In 1980, Republican Ronald Reagan surged ahead of incumbent Democratic president Jimmy Carter, by asking Americans during a debate: "It might be well if you ask yourself, are you better off than you were four years ago?" At the time the country was in an economic recession with high unemployment and inflation. Many Americans were not better off, and they responded to Reagan's question by electing him president.

More recently, some observers have criticized what they describe as media bias. Many conservatives argue that the media are generally more favorable to liberal candidates. Conservatives claim that most news stories routinely portray conservatives in a negative light. Many liberals, however, counter that the media are generally balanced. Liberals contend that the press is equally hard on all political groups. For instance, journalists vigorously investigated the Monica Lewinsky scandal in 1998, which led to the impeachment of liberal Democratic president Bill Clinton. In addition, some media, such as talk radio, are dominated by conservatives.

The authors in the following chapter explore the role of the media in presidential elections. The essays by historians, journalists, and other writers examine media bias and the influence of the press on voters, as well as the importance of presidential debates, in order to ascertain how great an impact the media have on the presidential election process.

Viewpoint 1

> "Never before have the establishment media cast aside the diaphanous veils of objectivity with such reckless self-revelation."

The Media Often Unfairly Favor One Candidate over Another

John O'Sullivan

In the viewpoint following, John O'Sullivan highlights media bias in the 2004 presidential election. O'Sullivan asserts that most media outlets actively sought to defeat George W. Bush in the presidential balloting and unfairly covered his campaign. The author centers his arguments around a series of examples of liberal bias, including efforts to discredit Bush's service in the Air National Guard during the Vietnam War. O'Sullivan is the editor in chief of United Press International and a former editor of National Review.

As you read, consider the following questions:

1. How has the rise of political blogs undermined the mainstream media, according to O'Sullivan?

John O'Sullivan, "The Limits of Media Bias: Try as They Might, They Couldn't Put Kerry over the Top," *National Review*, vol. 56, issue 22, November 29, 2004, p. 46.

2. What were the major problems with the CBS story on Bush's Air National Guard Service, in the author's opinion?
3. What were some of the other attacks on the Bush administration that O'Sullivan labels as unfair or biased?

[In 2004], Evan Thomas, *Newsweek's* Washington editor, conceded that there was media bias favoring Senator [John] Kerry and speculated that it might be worth a 15-point Democratic advantage. He later amended this estimate, to a mere 5-point advantage. If that second estimate is correct, the [George] Bush-[Dick] Cheney ticket would, on a level media playing field, have defeated Kerry-Edwards by a margin of 8 points. Given the outbreak of despair among Democrats occasioned by an actual 3-point loss, Terry McAuliffe and the entire [Democratic National Committee] would doubtless have committed mass hara-kiri [suicide] following Kerry's gracious concession over a glass of hemlock [poison].

It is almost certainly true that the Republican victory should have been larger. My own explanation for this shortfall, however, blames not the media, but President Bush—for failing to make 9/11 an occasion for reviving the traditional understanding of America as a melting pot, as opposed to various multicultural metaphors of salads and mosaics. Such a revival would have exactly matched the national mood of "United We Stand" and entrenched it for the long struggle against terrorism. And though the main purpose of such a cultural strategy would have been to strengthen America, it would also have aided the GOP [Republican Party] as a side-effect. Whether they realize it or not—and some of the Bush people seem to see it as a handicap—Republicans are the party of assimilation. Short of enlisting in the armed forces, voting Republican is just about the most assimilated thing an immigrant can do. And stressing the melting-pot concept might have won over entire classes of voters hitherto less concerned about either patriotism or national security. Unlike [Franklin Delano Roosevelt], however, President Bush made little attempt to turn a moment of patriotic unity into the permanent base for a large governing majority. Bush still won a majority of patriotic voters—including the "security moms"—but it could have been a larger vote and a larger victory.

Flagrant Bias

Against such a wave of patriotism, the media would have labored in vain. Indeed, they labored in vain against a much smaller wave. But labor they did. Never before have the establishment media cast aside the diaphanous veils of objectivity with such reckless self-revelation. Many "Republican-leaning" newspapers even removed, like [the biblical] Salome, that seventh veil concealing their firm liberal bias in news reporting—namely, the editorial endorsement of the Republican presidential candidate. It was with a heavy heart, liberal editorialists wrote, that they abandoned a century of tradition to conclude that George W. Bush was just too far out of the mainstream of modern America to endorse. With such bastions of Republicanism as the *Orlando* [FL] *Sentinel* switching to Kerry, it is hardly surprising that the national media were almost part of his campaign.

No doubt the Media Research Center will produce a detailed study of the flagrant media bias. My purpose here is to look at some outstanding examples of it and to ask why it failed to deliver a Kerry win. The first case—establishment-media coverage of the Swift-boat vets—is like the Sherlock Holmes story about the dog that barked in the night. Holmes realizes that the guard dog did not bark ... because the intruder was its owner! Similarly, when the Swift vets alleged that Kerry was unfit for command—because of his war-crimes allegations against U.S. soldiers in Vietnam, and his exaggerations of his own bravery there—the media failed to bark for a

Media Bias in Voting

In March and April 2005, the University of Connecticut's Department of Public Policy surveyed 300 journalists nationwide—120 who worked in the television industry and 180 who worked at newspapers and asked for whom they voted in the 2004 presidential election. In a report released May 16, 2005, the researchers disclosed that the journalists they surveyed selected Democratic challenger John Kerry over incumbent Republican President George W. Bush by a wide margin, 52 percent to 19 percent (with 1 percent choosing far-left independent candidate Ralph Nader). One out of five journalists (21 percent) refused to disclose their vote, while another six percent either didn't vote or said they did not know for whom they voted.

Media Research Center, "Media Bias Basics: How the Media Vote," 2005.

very long period. Then, when the silence became uncomfortable, it licked Kerry's hand. The *New York Times* ran a story to the effect that the Swift vets were a front for the Bush-[Karl] Rove campaign. Unfortunately, that compelled them to explain what this sinister front group was saying—so a number of media outlets tried to debunk the Swift-vet allegations. But the charges, overall, rang true—and stuck.

Big Media Failure

Why did the Big Media fail in this effort? In the first place, they no longer control the news agenda as completely as they did a decade ago. To be sure, the provincial press still follows the *Times*, the *Post, Time, Newsweek*, and the three networks as slavishly as ever—why do you think they're called provincial? But the Internet (which makes newspapers worldwide available), the bloggers, talk radio, and Fox News among them have a sufficiently large audience to force stories into the national consciousness even if they are shunned by what [social scientist] Paul Johnson calls the seven deadly sinners. It was owing to this alternative discussion of the Swift-vet allegations that *Unfit for Command* became a bestseller. Second, the bloggers—dismissed by one news executive as nerds sitting in front of their computers in pajamas—were more hard-nosed in their investigations and better informed in their analyses. The blogging community does not lack editors, it transpires; every blogger is an editor—and a fairly tough old-fashioned editor, at that: one intent on getting the facts right. News analyses in the major papers were repeatedly torn to shreds by the bloggers within hours. "Respected" columnists were laughed to scorn for their laziness in publishing pro-Kerry arguments that had been disproved online days before. It seemed the establishment media simply couldn't get it right—likely because, at some level, they believed the Swift vets and could not bear to look too closely into their claims. Whatever the cause, the coverage discredited the media more than it did the Swift vets.

Bush's National Guard Record

The same media that had shunned a sharp new story in that case were subsequently enthused by a battered old case of fraud: [News anchor] Dan Rather and CBS ware taken in by some forged documents purporting to show that George W. Bush, as a young man, had used his father's political pull to evade Vietnam by getting into the National Guard, lollygagging around while there and failing to obey a direct order to get a physical exam. Within minutes of the broadcast the fraud was detected by a blogger, and within two days—at most—it was generally accepted that Rather had been led up the garden path. The key moment came when [commentator] Terry McAuliffe speculated vaguely that if the documents were indeed fraudulent, then maybe [Bush frontman] Karl Rove was behind the whole scam. (Aha!)

Dan himself remained unwilling to concede.... And he produced a lady stenographer who had worked for the National Guard officer who in turn had not actually composed, written, or dictated the documents whose authenticity was in doubt (aha!) but who would have done so if he had been given the chance. She knew they represented his opinion of Bush, because she had typed similar documents about Bush for him. It was wonderfully reminiscent of the Jesuit debater's response to the argument that there was no evidence in the writing of the early Church fathers for his favorite doctrine: "Admittedly, there is no evidence in the writings of the fathers that have survived, but there is a mass of evidence in the documents that have perished." In the end, Dan was unable to get his hands on the documents that had perished and had to concede that the other documents in his possession could not be proved genuine.

False Documents

As the flames rose higher, however, he stuck to what he thought was the gravamen [significant part]: The documents may be false, but the story about Bush's lackadaisical National Guard record was true. It did not seem to occur to Rather and CBS that though every other news organization in the world might reasonably advance that claim, for them the story was the fraud: They had to acknowledge it without any self-justifying qualification. Above all, they could not use the excuse that the [London] *Daily Mirror* editor used to justify running fake photographs of British soldiers torturing Iraqis—namely, that the false evidence illustrated a larger truth. That is a manifestly inadequate argument in itself: Lies do not help establish truth. And it was given no serious additional support by the interviews that Dan conducted with other Texans claiming to have helped Bush—they all had possible partisan motives for discrediting the president and they were contradicted by other witnesses from that time. And what was the larger truth anyway?

The larger truth was that Bush was an idle, drunken, irresponsible wastrel as a young man. Well, so what? He tells us that all the time. As Mark Steyn pointed out, Rather and CBS were simply reiterating the life-affirming biography of the 43rd president: wasted youth, love of a good woman, demon drink forsworn, born again, serious husband and father, from the White House to the White House. Rather's scoop was no better than if he had produced a membership list of the East Houston Alcoholics Anonymous and pointed triumphantly to a scrawled signature that might be either "George W. Bush" or "Sonia N. Hunt." Unlike the Swift-vet allegations, which attacked a key Kerry argument, the Rather strike hit Bush like a congratulatory slap on the back: "You've come a long way, baby." What is revealing, however, is that Rather and CBS thought that it would damage the president—and for that reason were unwilling to admit defeat long after the corpse was buried.

Last-Minute Attacks

Journalists outside CBS may have sympathized, but they knew a lost cause when they saw it. They shuffled quickly away, muttering platitudes about journalistic ethics and proper sourcing. But CBS found an influential ally in a third case—namely, the last-minute surprise that wasn't, or the case of the missing munitions. Again, a simple storyline: An official of the IAEA [International Atomic Energy Agency] asks Iraq for information on munitions that had once been stored there; he is told that they can't be found—they have disappeared while under U.S. control; this reply is leaked to CBS and the *New York Times*; and CBS wishes to unveil the scoop two days before the election. A bout of journalistic ethics breaks out at the *Times*—which wants to run the story sooner so that 1) they will not both be scooped by other news outlets and 2) the administration will have a decent time to respond. The *Times* got its way.

The story probably damaged the Bush campaign somewhat, but the extra week allowed the following things to happen: All sorts of facts emerged to refute or at least to cloud the original story—they were removed before the U.S. arrived, they were removed by the U.S. after we arrived, they're still there, and so on, until everyone is thoroughly confused.

Finally, deprived of its #1 October Surprise, CBS's *60 Minutes* ran a story about how National Guard units in Iraq lack vital equipment such as armored vehicles and bullets. This was a serious and important story. If it was intended to damage Bush, however, it was wide of the mark, because its focus was mainly on congressional misallocation of defense spending for "pork," and because Kerry voted against the $87 billion allocation for Iraq. So the media campaign ended not with a surprise but with a badly aimed bang.

The short moral of all these episodes: For the media: Throw fewer boomerangs. For the Democrats: Friends don't let friends drive wearing blinkers. And for the Republicans who deal with the media: Buy a dog.

VIEWPOINT 2

> *"Research has shown that the news media aren't consistently biased against any political party."*

Media Coverage of Candidates Is Generally Balanced

Pam Frost Gorder

In the following viewpoint, Pam Frost Gorder details the results of a study on media bias. She relates that popular perceptions that the media unfairly target one party or individual candidates is incorrect and that, instead, most coverage of presidential candidates or major issues is relatively balanced. However, people see bias when coverage does not reflect their views. Gorder is a science writer and freelance journalist who writes about a variety of topics.

As you read, consider the following questions:

1. Are Republicans or Democrats more likely to think the media are biased in their political coverage, according to Gorder?
2. How do politicians attempt to use perceptions of media bias to their advantage, in the author's opinion?

Pam Frost Gorder, "Think Political News Is Biased? Depends Who You Ask," *The Ohio State University Research News*, April 7, 2003. http://researchnews.osu.edu. Reproduced by permission.

3. What is the "hostile media phenomenon," according to Gorder?

Are the news media politically biased against people with "your" beliefs? If you're a Republican, your answer depends on who you talk to, and how often.

That's the finding of a [2007] Ohio State University study: Republicans who frequently talk politics with other Republicans are more likely to believe that the so-called "liberal media" are biased against them than are Republicans who talk with like-minded people less often.

The same didn't hold true for Democrats in the study, whose feelings about media bias didn't differ based on who they talked to. Engaging in frequent political debates with people who hold opposing beliefs didn't have an effect on either Democrats or Republicans.

Study on Media Bias

"When we judge whether news coverage is biased, we must have some kind of baseline in mind—a perception of what is fair and balanced coverage. This study shows that our conversational contacts influence our baseline," said William P. Eveland, coauthor of the study and assistant professor of journalism and communication at Ohio State. The results appear in the March [2007] issue of the journal *Political Psychology*.

The study asked some 3,000 participants whether they identify with a political party, and how often they talk about politics generally and specifically with very conservative or very liberal people.

"People who talk with a set of contacts biased in their favor develop an unrealistic notion of what is fair and balanced," he said.

Eveland and his coauthor, Dhavan V. Shah of the University of Wisconsin–Madison, suspect that Republicans' current perception of media bias stems in part from actual media re-

Conservatives More Likely to See Media Bias

The vast majority of American voters believe media bias is alive and well—83% of likely voters said the media is biased in one direction or another, while just 11% believe the media doesn't take political sides, a [2007] IPDI/Zogby Interactive poll shows....

Nearly two-thirds of those online respondents who detected bias in the media (64%) said the media leans left, while slightly more than a quarter of respondents (28%) said they see a conservative bias on their TV sets and in their column inches....

While 97% of Republicans surveyed said the media are liberal, two-thirds of political independents feel the same, but fewer than one in four independents (23%) said they saw a conservative bias. Democrats, while much more likely to perceive a conservative bias than other groups, were not nearly as sure the media was against them as were the Republicans. While Republicans were unified in their perception of a left-wing media, just two-thirds of Democrats were certain the media skewed right—and 17% said the bias favored the left.

Zogby International Poll, March 14, 2007.

porting of claims of a bias against conservatives. George H. W. Bush's 1992 campaign slogan "Annoy the media—re-elect Bush" is just one instance of these claims, and news coverage of them. Claims of media bias against Bill Clinton in the 1992 presidential campaign and leading up to his impeachment demonstrate that Democrats often claim media bias, too, Eveland said.

Politicians and Media Bias

Politicians may be using perceptions of media bias to their advantage. "The individuals charging bias may have an agenda that leads them to make such claims in order to coerce more favorable coverage from a press that prides itself on objectivity," Eveland said.

"Research has shown that the news media aren't consistently biased against any political party, yet the perception persists," he added.

He and Shah surveyed participants in June 2000, when political news coverage of candidates for the 2000 presidential election was fresh in Americans' minds.

People were asked to rate their agreement with the statement "Most news media are biased against my views," on a scale of 1 (definitely disagree) to 6 (definitely agree). Democrats' responses averaged 3.2, or essentially only weak disagreement with the statement. Republicans averaged from 3.6 to 4.2, with those who engaged in frequent conversations with other Republicans tending to agree even more.

The study also supports the existence of what researchers call the "hostile media phenomenon," Eveland said. People who are highly committed, regardless of their specific views—such as those who are strong partisans on either side or those actively involved in politics—will perceive a generally balanced news story to be biased in favor of their opponents.

As to why Democrats' conversations didn't change their perceptions, he suspects that the notion of media bias is stronger among Republicans because of more frequent bias claims among Republican elites, and so the concept is simply reinforced more in personal conversations.

While he and Shah have no immediate plans to expand this study in the future, Eveland said the same ideas probably apply to Americans' attitude about news coverage of the war in Iraq. "People who are staunchly pro-war would think that most coverage is anti-war," and vice versa, he said.

VIEWPOINT 3

> *"The assault began in July 2003, when Joseph Wilson accused the president [George W. Bush] of lying."*

The Media Often Distort Candidates' Positions

Stephen F. Hayes

In the following viewpoint, Stephen F. Hayes examines major instances of media bias in the 2004 presidential election. Hayes explores four major examples of bias and several less significant cases. He contends that the media undertook a concerted effort to defeat President George W. Bush because of a general mistrust of his administration and widespread suspicion of Bush's view of the world. Hayes concludes that the media support provided Bush's opponent John Kerry with many additional votes on election day. Hayes is a writer for the Weekly Standard.

As you read, consider the following questions:

1. Why did many reporters favor Kerry over Bush in the 2004 presidential election, according to Hayes?
2. What were some of the major examples of media bias cited by the author in the 2004 balloting?

Stephen F. Hayes, "The Other Losers Tuesday Night: The Failed Media Effort to Oust George W. Bush," *Weekly Standard*, vol. 10, November 15, 2004, pp. 15–16.

3. What impact does Hayes believe the media had on the voting in 2004?

"We'd rather be last than wrong." So said Dan Rather anchoring election night coverage for CBS. He was apparently serious. That he could say this with a straight face only weeks after presenting the world with forged documents to bring down the president should cement his reputation as the least trusted man in America.

Dan Rather is just a small part of a much bigger story. His careless reporting and, later, dogmatic defense of his errors were but one episode in the media's long offensive against George W. Bush.

The assault began in July 2003, when Joseph Wilson accused the president of lying. Wilson's charges have since been thoroughly discredited and the author of *The Politics of Truth* revealed as unreliable. But the damage was done. Wilson's claim that the Bush administration had knowingly cooked intelligence provided the prism through which many reporters viewed the election.

For some 16 months, then, journalists at the *New York Times* and the *Washington Post* and the television networks saw themselves not as conveyors of facts but as truth-squadders, toiling away on the gray margins of political debate to elucidate the many misstatements, exaggerations, and outright lies of the Bush administration and its campaign affiliates. Sometimes these "fact-check" pieces were labeled "news analysis." More often, they were splashed on the front page as straight news or presented on the evening news.

Media Distortions

Many of these reporters were trained at the best universities in the country. They fancy themselves *thinkers*, not mere scribes. They go to work every day to tell us not what the Bush administration has said, but what it has left unsaid. They are scornful of the president's "simple" worldview—where Americans are good and terrorists are evil, where nations are with us or against us—and suspicious of his motives. They inhabit a world where Bush administration policymakers are incapable of telling the truth and "intelligence officials," especially those who provide them leaks, are unimpeachable. They knew that the Bush campaign lied more than the Kerry campaign and that when the Kerry campaign lied it was of little or no consequence.

Think I'm exaggerating? Consider the memo written some three weeks before the election by ABC News political director Mark Halperin.

"[T]he current Bush attacks on Kerry involve distortions and taking things out of context in a way that goes beyond what Kerry has done," Halperin wrote. As a consequence, ABC has "a responsibility to hold both sides accountable to the public interest, but that doesn't mean we reflexively and artificially hold both sides 'equally' accountable when the facts don't warrant that.... It's up to Kerry to defend himself, of course. But as one of the few news organizations with the skill and strength to help voters evaluate what the candidates are saying to serve the public interest [*sic*]. Now is the time for all of us to step up and do that right."

Halperin was way behind. His colleagues had been on the job for months. Here is a brief, random review of their effort.

Joseph Wilson When Wilson claimed that his clandestine work proved the Bush administration was lying about alleged Iraqi attempts to procure uranium from Niger, he was lionized as a courageous truthteller willing to stand up to a corrupt and deceitful administration. Oops. In fact, the bipartisan Senate Intelligence Committee review of pre-Iraq war intelligence concluded that Wilson's findings contradicted his earlier public claims and that despite his insistence that his wife, undercover CIA operative Valerie Plame, had had nothing to do

2003 Survey Reflects Public Mistrust of *New York Times*, Mainstream Media

The data reflects more than a generalized distrust of media reporting. The *Wall Street Journal*, CNN, Fox News Channel, and local newspapers all were seen as significantly more reliable than the *Times*.

All Adults	Reliable	Not Reliable	Net
Fox News	72%	14%	+58%
Local Newspaper	73%	21%	+52%
Wall Street Journal	59%	11%	+48%
CNN	66%	21%	+45%
NY Times	46%	23%	+23%

TAKEN FROM: Rassmussen Reports, "Just 46% Consider NY Times Reliable," July 16, 2003. www.rassmussenreports.com.

with his selection, his work was undertaken after she recommended him for the job. The media buried those reports.

Richard Clarke Clarke, a former White House counterterrorism czar, was similarly celebrated when he published a book criticizing the Bush administration's conduct of the war on terror and the Iraq war. The Fox News Channel released a transcript of a background briefing Clarke gave while he was still at the White House in which Clarke praised some of the very efforts he would later criticize. Most journalists focused on the propriety of Fox's action, not the contradictions in Clarke's accounts. Clarke also argued that Iraq had never supported [terrorist group] al Qaeda, "ever." Several months later, the final 9/11 Commission report, however, quoted an email Clarke had written in 1999 in which he cited the existence of an agreement between Iraq and al Qaeda as evidence that [former Iraqi dictator] Saddam Hussein had assisted al Qaeda with chemical weapons. Most journalists ignored the revelation.

Dan Rather The CBS anchor aired a story about "new" documents suggesting that the young George W. Bush had received preferential treatment from political big-wigs to avoid serving in the Vietnam war. The documents were forged—something CBS had been warned about *before* the story was broadcast. When numerous forensic document experts concluded that the memos were fraudulent. Rather lashed out at his critics as partisan hacks and spoke of the supposed broader truth of the allegations. Although CBS later backed away from the story, Rather never apologized to President Bush.

The Missing Explosives

Eight days before Election Day the *New York Times* published a major story about missing high explosives in Iraq. The *Times*'s account was based largely on an erroneous assessment from IAEA [International Atomic Energy Agency] chief Mohamed El Baradei. The *Times* collaborated on the piece with *60 Minutes*, and a producer from CBS admitted that they had hoped to hold the story for October 31—two days before voters would go to the polls.

These are some of the big ones. There are dozens of smaller examples. Knight-Ridder newspapers reported that President Bush had claimed an "operational" relationship between Iraq and al Qaeda in a speech he delivered in Tennessee. He had said nothing close. The *Washington Post* omitted a key phrase from one of Vice President Dick Cheney's appearances on *Meet the Press*, an omission that inverted his meaning. And on it goes.

The Pro-Kerry Press

Evan Thomas, a veteran correspondent for *Newsweek*, offered a refreshingly candid assessment of the impact of a pro-Kerry media before the election, saying it could provide the Massachusetts setts senator with a 15-point bump. Thomas later revised this estimate down to 5 points. There's no way to know, of course, but I believe his first guess was more accurate.

What does all of this mean? Will there be a postelection rapprochement?

We're not off to a good start. Minutes after President Bush thanked the country for electing him to a second term, Mark Halperin, author of the ABC memo, called the president a "lame duck."

Here we go again.

VIEWPOINT 4

"[Newspapers] and the traditional media can present the news objectively, and ... there's a marketplace for the objective presentation of news."

Media Coverage of Candidates Is Objective

Matt Welch

In this viewpoint, Matt Welch discusses objectivity among journalists and news outlets. He presents arguments from the 2004 presidential election that the media were biased but concludes that traditional, objective reporting will continue to be the cornerstone of media coverage of presidential elections. Welch also examines the rise of "new media" sources such as the Internet. Welch is an associate editor for Reason *and a columnist for the Canadian newspaper the* National Post.

As you read, consider the following questions:

1. Why did photographer Luis Sinco leave Iraq, according to Welch?
2. What three factors are likely to continue the dominance of the traditional media, in the author's opinion?

Matt Welch, "That Old, Tired Balancing Act: Did the Election Kill Objective Campaign Journalism?" *Reason*, vol. 36, issue 9, February 2005, pp. 16–17.

3. What does the success of Fox News, as well as non-traditional media, mean for the news market, according to Welch?

Jay Rosen, chair of the Journalism Department at New York University, calls it "The Contraption." Thomas Lang, a correspondent for CampaignDesk.org, terms it the "automatic pilot approach to reporting." [Journalist] Hunter S. Thompson labels it "the Objective rules and dogma," adding that it's "one of the main reasons American politics has been allowed to be so corrupt for so long." More politely, *A Free and Responsible Press*, the influential 1947 report prepared by an all-star cast of 13 academics, referred to it as the means by which reporters pursue "a truthful, comprehensive, and intelligent account of the day's events in a context which gives them meaning."

By whatever name, the ethic by which the vast majority of daily newspapers and network news broadcasts have produced their work in the last half-century has come under a perhaps unprecedentedly heavy barrage of questioning by self-doubting journalists in the wake of George [W.] Bush's re-election. From *New York Times* columnist Thomas Friedman, who awoke November 3 [2004] feeling "deeply troubled" about his countrymen, to *Los Angeles Times* photographer Luis Sinco, who abruptly left Iraq because of the election's "clear-cut signal" that "we as journalists are not changing anybody's mind about this conflict," reporters seemed to take the results as a personal repudiation, requiring immediate reassessment.

A few of the many examples [from late 2004]:

October 24. "We journalists, we are at sea," former *New York Times* reporter Doug McGill writes on mcgillreport.org, "because our Grand Old Professional Code is falling to pieces."

October 30. "There's a growing sense that this race may involve tectonic shifts in the landscape of political journalism," predicts *Los Angeles Times* media columnist Tim Rutten.

November 12. "We are moving away from a model of objective reporting," Alex Jones, director of Harvard's Joan Shorenstein Center on the Press, Politics, and Public Policy, warns in a speech. "We are moving from partisanship to something much worse." The same day, *National Journal* columnist William Powers tells *The Hartford Courant*, "There is so much change happening, and everyone feels a little lost and disoriented."

Jay Rosen crystallized the debate on November 3 with the provocative suggestion that some media outlets currently in the Objective camp might switch to a self-consciously Oppositional stance, treating the Bush administration more like [conservative commentator] Rush Limbaugh treats [Sen.] Hillary Clinton.

"The contraption [mainstream journalism] as for explaining, situating and defending itself has in 2004 finally broken down, given out after 40 years of heavy, reliable use," Rosen wrote on his weblog, at pressthink.org. "I believe Big Journalism cannot respond as it would in previous years: with bland vows to cover the Administration fairly and a firm intention to make no changes whatsoever in its basic approach to politics and news. The situation is too unstable, the world is changing too rapidly, and political journalism has been pretending for too long that an old operating system will last forever."

A Media Revolution

Is a media revolution really in the air? If you ask the people who, unlike everyone quoted above, are downright cheerful about Bush's victory and Fox's dominance of the cable news ratings, the answer is a robust "Hell, yes!" On one side, new media with new styles are booming; on the other, credibility crises have kneecapped such previously authoritative institutions as CBS News, *The New York Times*, and the BBC. Former [Ronald] Reagan speechwriter Peggy Noonan encapsulated that spirit in a November 4 *Wall Street Journal* column: "Every time the big networks and big broadsheet national newspapers

Blogs and Subjective Reporting

In the blogging world, anyone producing an online diary or Web site that collects commentary from around the Internet is supposed to let everyone know his or her politics. The theory: Web surfers need to know bloggers' biases to understand their motivations. Presenting both sides of an issue in the interest of fairness isn't required.

"Objectivity is a worthwhile objective, but it needs to be recognized that it can't be reached," [blogger David] Weinberger said.

Mark Memmott, USA Today, *July 26, 2006.*

tried to pull off a bit of pro-liberal mischief—CBS and the fabricated Bush National Guard documents, the *New York Times* and bombgate, CBS's *60 Minutes*' attempting to coordinate the breaking of bombgate on the Sunday before the election—the yeomen of the blogosphere and AM radio and the Internet took them down."

But there are three good reasons to be skeptical that November 3 sounded the death knell for old-style political journalism. First, every presidential election since 1960, if not earlier, has been followed by increasingly louder whither-journalism sessions. It was only [in 2000] that the major networks and newspapers were vowing never again to get bamboozled by Election Day exit polls. Needless to say, such fretting does not always produce reforms.

Second, while the New Media revolution has unleashed a boom in publishing outlets and has converted news consumers into news producers, it has yet to create a style of reporting dominant enough to replace that which it so successfully criticizes.

Niche publishing has nibbled off chunks of the mainstream media's audience: Since 1996 the percentage of consumers who use newspapers as their primary source of campaign news has dropped from 60 to 46, while the percentage who mainly use the Internet has grown from 3 to 21, according to an October [2004] survey by the Pew Research Center. But newspaper publishing and television news are still two of the most lucrative business models in the country.

The Dominance of Mainstream Media

Which leads to the most important reason for skepticism: inertia. For the last half-century, despite the growth and success of niche publishing, professional journalism has had one dominant paradigm, one that has allowed its owners to get spectacularly rich and its workers to make out all right as well. No matter how rattled reporters seemed in November, change from within will come incrementally, not instantly. Rather than tear up the old reporting model, news outlets are gingerly experimenting with some of the New Media's more successful strategies: publishing weblogs, introducing greater transparency, encouraging a more subjective writing style.

"I had a publisher here once who said that you hunt where the ducks are flying," says John Robinson, editor of the 100,000-circulation *News Record* of Greensboro, North Carolina. "And the ducks seem to be flying online."

In August 2004, Robinson started a weblog (blog.newsrecord.com/jrblog) where he engages readers in a more direct and interactive way than in his existing weekly column. *The News & Record* is also trying to become a hub for more opinionated local bloggers, a strategy that has been adopted as well by newspapers from California to New Jersey.

Subjective Journalism?

But that doesn't necessarily foreshadow subjective campaign coverage, or a policy of asking reporters to 'fess up their biases. "I'm not to that point yet," Robinson says. "I still believe that newspapers and the traditional media can present the news objectively, and that there's a marketplace for the objective presentation of news."

As the success of Fox News, political talk radio, partisan book publishing, and blogging has shown, there's a healthy marketplace for nonobjective presentation as well. So [far] though, subjectivity has flourished only in markets that are competitive, such as New York newspapers or cable news.

With entry costs plummeting for all forms of media—more than 50 daily newspapers have been launched in the U.S. this young century—competition looks set to flourish even in currently uncompetitive markets. But as long as Objective publishing remains profitable, the two sides of the media divide are likely to dig deeper trenches. Anxious professionals on one side will continue to take the Contraption to the bank, while the barbarian army outside grows in numbers and weapons.

Jay Rosen and others are predicting that some exasperated member of the Old Guard will switch sides before 2008 and come out politically—if it's not too late to recapture their eroding audience. When and if that day comes, a generation of media critics will have to grapple with a new problem: What if the liberal media finally decide to become the liberal media?

"Some day," Rosen wrote in November [2004], "a clever historian is going to explain how fear of being politicized (legitimate) convinced American journalists that the press could have—and should have no politics at all. (Not legitimate.) It has been one devastating illusion."

VIEWPOINT 5

> *"These closed, two-candidate debates are nothing more than a disguised corporate contribution to the two parties that run national government."*

Presidential Debates Limit Choice and Exclude Third Parties

Jamin B. Raskin

In the following viewpoint, Jamin B. Raskin criticizes the current system of presidential debates. He specifically condemns the Commission on Presidential Debates for its ties to corporate America and its arbitrary rules that discourage participation by third-party candidates. Raskin calls for a return to the more open and free debates that marked past presidential elections. Raskin is a professor of constitutional law at the American University and is the head of the Appleseed Project on Electoral Reform.

As you read, consider the following questions:

1. How does the Commission on Presidential Debates stifle participation by third parties, in Raskin's opinion?

Jamin B. Raskin, "Let's Take Back the Debates! Commission on Presidential Debates Biased, Exclusionary," *The Nation*, vol. 270, issue 5, Febrary 7, 2000, p. 21.

2. What is the relationship between the Commission on Presidential Debates and its corporate sponsors, according to the author?
3. What criteria do candidates have to meet in order to be eligible to participate in presidential debates, according to Raskin?

If Jesse Ventura had been excluded from the Minnesota gubernatorial debates in 1998, he almost certainly would have lost his run for governor. But the Reform Party nominee—a giant, bald, all-pro wrestler derided by the state establishment as frivolous and unelectable—was invited to participate in the eight televised debates of that campaign, and by the end of these spirited discussions, Minnesotans concluded that Ventura had far more ambitious plans for their state than did the two-party-system retreads he trounced on Election Day.

At the presidential level, where campaigns have been subsumed by private wealth and corporate power, the suggestion that general-election debates be opened up to outsider-candidates and citizen questioners is considered heretical. Presidential debates are designed not as the focal point in a broad public dialogue among our divergent political forces—Democratic, Republican, Independent, Reform, Libertarian, Green—but as a ritual celebration of the two-party system and its incestuous marriage to corporate capital. In every pundit's revealing metaphor, debates are the "Super Bowl of American politics," a bipartisan campaign commercial brought to you by corporate sponsors who profit from America's money politics regardless of which team prevails on Election Day.

The official organizer is the Commission on Presidential Debates (CPD), which was set up by the Democratic and Republican National Committees [DNC and RNC] in 1987 to oust the League of Women Voters, which had the temerity to invite Independent John Anderson to debate in 1980 and refused to be a marionette for the two parties. Despite its recent appalling insistence that it is "nonpartisan," the CPD was launched as an avowedly "bipartisan" corporation "to implement joint sponsorship of general election presidential and vice-presidential debates ... by the national Republican and Democratic Committees between their respective nominees." It has been chaired continuously by Frank Fahrenkopf Jr. and Paul Kirk Jr., the former national Republican and Democratic Party chairs and powerhouse lawyer/lobbyists. The debate commission has been scrupulously divided ever since between Democratic and Republican Party loyalists.

The CPD and Ross Perot

With truly comic solemnity, the CPD in 1996 made a show of pretending to consult a long list of arbitrary and manipulable "factors" to decide whether Ross Perot was "electable" and therefore eligible to debate. The fact that he was on the ballot in fifty states and the District of Columbia, had won 19 percent of the vote in 1992 and had received nearly $30 million in public funds to run was deemed insignificant. The key factors were the "professional opinions of the Washington bureau chiefs of major newspapers, news magazines, and broadcast networks," the "opinions of a comparable group of professional campaign managers and pollsters not then employed by the candidates under consideration" and the "published views of prominent political commentators."

When the CPD excluded Perot and the Green Party's Ralph Nader, it meant that the two pro-NAFTA [North American Free Trade Agreement] pro-GATT [General Agreement on Tariffs and Trade], pro-corporate, soft-money candidates were left to debate in peace while the anti-Establishment candidates, Perot and Nader, were branded "unelectable." When you declare certain candidates "not viable," you of course guarantee their nonviability and facilitate a conspiracy of silence on key issues.

The Mission of the CPD

The Commission on Presidential Debates (CPD) was established in 1987 to ensure that debates, as a permanent part of every general election, provide the best possible information to viewers and listeners. Its primary purpose is to sponsor and produce debates for the United States presidential and vice presidential candidates and to undertake research and educational activities relating to the debates. The organization, which is a nonprofit, nonpartisan corporation, sponsored all the presidential debates in 1988, 1992, 2000 and 2004.

Commission on Presidential Debates, "Our Mission," 2004.

The CPD's governance-by-pundits is such an affront to democracy that it is almost a relief to read the proceedings of a post-election conference at Harvard's Institute of Politics, which tell the true story of how an old-fashioned back-room political conspiracy actually shut the door on Perot in 1996. Explaining that the Clinton campaign "wanted the debates to be a nonevent," George Stephanopoulos, then a senior adviser to the President, detailed the dynamics of excluding Perot: "[The Bob Dole campaign] didn't have leverage going into the negotiations. They were behind, they needed to make sure Perot wasn't in it. As long as we could agree to Perot not being in it we could get everything else we wanted going in. We got our time frame, we got our length, we got our moderator."

Corporate Interests

Although the CPD is well-known as a front group for the two parties, its enmeshment with corporate America is more obscure. The CPD has operated over the years by collecting millions of dollars in contributions from large corporations, which not only receive in return bundles of free debate tickets, receptions, trinkets and access to the candidates but also selective exposure to the American public. In 1992, after pumping into the debates some $250,000 in cash and in-kind contributions, Philip Morris won the right to hang a "large banner visible during post-debate interviews." It should have read: "The 1992 American presidential campaign, brought to you by the cancer industry."

Today's electoral-industrial complex is so tightly constructed that the same corporate interests bankrolling the CPD—which purports to make objective decisions on who should participate in the debates—also pump millions in soft money directly into Democratic and Republican coffers. Anheuser-Busch, a proud debate sponsor in 1992 and 1996, has given more than a million dollars in soft money directly to the DNC and RNC [1996–2000]. The corporate "king of beer" recently announced that, having given $550,000 to the CPD, it would be the "sole sponsor" of the presidential debate in St. Louis this year. Perennial debate sponsor Philip Morris gave more than $3 million to the two parties in 1996. Bank of America poured hundreds of thousands of dollars that year into the coffers of both major parties and the debates that advertised their candidates.

The Federal Election Commission

If the Federal Election Commission (FEC) had not itself been captured by the campaign industry, it could have blown the whistle on this outrageous corporate subsidization and promotion of two parties over the others. After all, federal election law categorically forbids corporate expenditures and contributions in federal elections, and these closed, two-candidate debates are nothing more than a disguised corporate contribution to the two parties that run national government. The blending of private corporate power with public elections is precisely the evil forbidden by the Federal Election Campaign Act.

Responding to a 1996 complaint by Ross Perot's campaign committee, Lawrence Noble, general counsel of the FEC, issued a report in 1998 finding "reason to believe" that the 1996 debates themselves constituted illegal campaign contributions and that the CPD was operating as an illegal "political committee" on behalf of the two major parties. Noble, who should be declared whistleblower of the nineties, wrote: "The role played by Clinton/Gore and Dole/Kemp in CPD's debate participant selection process and the role played by the DNC and the RNC in the creation of CPD suggest that CPD's major purpose may be to facilitate the election of either of the major parties' candidates for president."

But when Noble turned his report in to the FEC commissioner—Democrats and Republicans themselves appointed in a strictly bipartisan (and constitutionally dubious) manner—they unanimously voted to reject their own general counsel's conclusions. Citing the objectivity of the "pool of experts" consulted in the CPD's process, the FEC gave its blessing to the CPD's manipulable and tautological "electability" screen for debate participation.

The 2000 Debates

In 2000 the debate issue could [have] blow[n] right open. Every public opinion poll done in 1996 showed huge majorities of the American people supporting the right of Perot to debate and registering disapproval of his exclusion. Public figures across the spectrum, even conservatives like [journalist] George Will, are rebelling at the naked manipulation of public opinion through debate gerrymandering. The anarchic spirit of the Internet age is prepared to collide with the closed debates choreographed by the CPD.

In response to the 1996 debacle, the CPD has set a new criterion for debate participation: Candidates must average 15 percent support in five national public opinion polls a week before each debate. Amazingly, the CPD announced that it would be up to the pollsters themselves to decide whether to include third-party candidates in their polling questions. Thus, if two of the five polling organizations decided not to list hypothetical Green candidate Ralph Nader (most pollsters omitted him in 1996) and he therefore came in at zero, he would need to average 25 percent in the other three to make the cut. Of course, polls are famously skewed against outsiders from the start, and many people refuse to tell pollsters the truth: No pollster predicted Ventura would win, for example.

At any rate, the CPD is asking the wrong question. The relevant question is not, "Whom do you think you would vote for today before the debate has even taken place?" It is, "Whom do you want to see included in the debate so you can decide what the important issues are and to help clarify your choices and thoughts?" Yet the CPD, which purports to act in the public interest, would never touch this approach. As much as 76 percent of the public said Perot should be invited to debate in 1996, which gives you a sense of how dangerous procedural democracy would be to the guardians of rigged debate.

The CPD's arbitrary 15 percent polling figure is triple the statutory 5 percent that a new party needs to have collected in a presidential election for federal public funding of a subsequent campaign. Where does the CPD get the right to override not only federal law but constitutional democracy? Rule-by-pollsters defeats the whole idea of a campaign, which the CPD seems not to understand is more than just a mathematical contest over who will win. It is the way we float new political ideas and change public opinion. Abe Lincoln lost his campaign for the Senate against Stephen Douglas in 1858, but the program he spelled out in their famous debates captured the nation's imagination and led to his election as President two years later—on the relatively new Republican Party ticket at that.

New Debate Criteria

It would not be hard to design both new debate-invitation criteria and a new commission that would broaden democratic discussion and still prevent the dread "cacophony" that the CPD constantly invokes (a problem that does not trouble Democratic and Republican managers when it takes place within their party primaries, as witnessed in numerous New Hampshire debates that have included Steve Forbes, George W. Bush, John McCain, Alan Keyes, Orrin Hatch and Gary Bauer). There should be two or three criteria for candidates to receive a debate invitation: The candidate should be (1) constitutionally eligible to serve as President; (2) on the ballot in a sufficient number of states—which takes hundreds of thousands of signatures—such that the candidate could actually collect a majority in the Electoral College; and (3), if the prior two criteria would produce more than five candidates, reasonably likely to affect the outcome of the election or to advance public discourse.

This last criterion is obviously open to interpretation, so the key question becomes who will be applying the criteria. Right now we have a commission of people selected for their service and loyalty to two parties purporting to speak for all Americans. There are no Independents, no Greens, no Reform Party members, no Libertarians involved. In other words, one-third of the public has no representation in this body. If we all agree that the debates should be held in the interests of the American people, why not develop a process that reflects all of the people?

A Reform Model

Let us return to the old-fashioned American institution of the grand jury and invite twenty-three American citizens chosen at random to come together to deliberate and invite presidential candidates to debate. They could also choose the moderators and questioners, who do not have to be journalists. Why not also union leaders, university presidents, businesspeople, historians? Why not the citizen-members of this grand jury themselves? Everyone remembers [news anchor] Bernard Shaw asking Michael Dukakis in 1988 whether he would favor the death penalty for a man who raped his wife. The Democrat's wooden response sealed his fate. But Shaw could also have asked the pro-life George [H.W.] Bush whether, if his wife or daughter were raped, he would insist on her bringing a resulting pregnancy to term.

If there is any hope of derailing a corporate takeover of [future] election[s], our much-celebrated but underutilized "civil society" in the United States—the universities, foundations, unions and civic groups—must stand up and reclaim our debates and our campaigns. One of the wonderful things about the Lincoln-Douglas debates was the spirited interaction between the audience and the candidates, complete with cheers, jeers and well-timed heckling. It is a measure of our democratic disempowerment today that the American people are completely passive spectators in our presidential debates, consumers of a controlled corporate spectacle that wears our expectations like an armored suit and may as well be offering us a choice between Budweiser and Bud Light.

VIEWPOINT 6

> *"The perceived winners of presidential debates, in every case since the first one ... have always gone on to win the presidency."*

Presidential Debates Are an Important Component of the Election Process

Richard Shenkman

In the following viewpoint, Richard Shenkman reviews highlights from the twentieth-century presidential debates that were televised. The author discusses which qualities make a candidate more likely to win debates and how individual candidates made costly mistakes that often ended their chances of victory. Underscoring his examples is his contention that the debates continue to be an important part of the election process. Shenkman is the editor of the History News Network and the author of the book Presidential Ambition.

As you read, consider the following questions:

1. What personality trait does the winner of presidential debates usually possess, according to Shenkman?

Richard Shenkman, "Presidential Debates: How They've Changed History," *Tompaine .com*, October 1, 2000. Reproduced by permission.

2. What mistake during the 1976 presidential debate cost Gerald Ford the election, in the author's opinion?
3. What response hurt Michael Dukakis in the 1988 presidential debate, as cited by Shenkman?

Serious Opinion Makers in Washington dismiss the [presidential] debates as so much Hollywood showmanship. The debates, Elizabeth Drew has complained, "tend to reward wrong or irrelevant qualifications." Furthermore: "The talents called forth—being quick on one's feet, memorizing the better responses, hiring the better writer of one-liners—have little to do with what we need in a president."

She might have added that because they are primarily television events debates place a premium on television values, giving a prime advantage to the person who seems more likeable. This, I suspect, is what really bothers Serious Opinion Makers. TV debates trivialize politics.

Admission: I agree [television commercial icon] Mr. Whipple is appealing; I don't think that means we should invite him to change his residence to 1600 Pennsylvania Avenue. But the people who hate TV and what it's done to American politics—and one of the things it's done is to make niceness a qualification for the presidency miss the fact that niceness is essential in the Television Age if a president is to command the following of the American people. And the ability to attract followers is, like it or not, a primary test of a president....

And debates are as good a measure of this quality as we have. Ronald Reagan had it; [presidential also-rans] Michael Dukakis and Walter Mondale did not.

This is one reason, why [debates are] important. [They] clarify who ... can attract followers.

Debates and Presidential Winners

Another is that the perceived winners of presidential debates, in every case since the first one held [in 1960] have always gone on to win the presidency. [John] Kennedy, [Jimmy] Carter, [Ronald] Reagan, [George H.W.] Bush, [Bill] Clinton ... each was generally regarded as the over-all winner in the presidential debates that occurred during the year in which they were elected.

In 1960 Kennedy, relaxed, witty and tan, easily beat Nixon, who, especially in the first debate, came across as awkward, insincere, and tired. As an Atlanta columnist put it, Nixon looked like a "salesman of cemetery plots." Though Nixon made a better impression in the subsequent three debates, what happened in the first was what lingered in the pubic consciousness, defining him in ways he found he never could escape. Deciding to debate Kennedy, it turned out, was the worst political miscalculation Nixon made that year. Asked a few weeks later why he agreed, he couldn't come up with an answer. He himself had argued earlier against debating Kennedy. "In 1946, a damn fool incumbent named Jerry Voorhis debated a young lawyer and it cost him the election," Nixon had told staffers. But when the networks made the offer to host a debate, Nixon, perhaps feeling that his manhood was at stake, found he couldn't bring himself to refuse.

In the next presidential debate in 1976, Carter easily bested [incumbent Gerald] Ford, who is remembered for making the bizarre declaration that Poland wasn't under Soviet domination. It was the first time a gaffe contributed to the defeat of a candidate. Ford said afterward he didn't even realize at the time that he'd made a gaffe. He had and it was serious. As a result of a brief exchange with a reporter, he had instantly thrown away the key edge he had over Carter, his experience as an incumbent president and the presumption that he knew more than the challenger about running the country.

Ronald Reagan

In 1980 Carter found himself up against a real pro, the former star of the General Electric Theater. Ronald Reagan demon-

strated repeatedly in his encounters why politicians hated to share the same stage with him. (After an encounter in 1967 [presidential candidate] Robert Kennedy groused to an aide as he made his exit, "Don't ever put me on with that sonofabitch again.") Carter attempted to show that Reagan was a scary warmonger, but it was Carter who frightened people when he claimed, in his notorious answer to a question about nuclear weapons, that he consulted his teenage daughter Amy for advice. "I had a discussion with Amy the other day before I came here, to ask her what the most important issue was. She said she thought nuclear weaponry and the control of nuclear arms [was]."

When Carter accused Reagan of wanting to cut the Medicare program, Reagan famously cocked his head, in a moment that had been scripted during rehearsals, "There you go again." Carter never recovered from the crack. In his closing remarks Reagan successfully shifted the nature of the election. Carter until then had succeeded in making Reagan's competence to hold the presidency the critical question facing voters. In a few sentences Reagan turned the election into a referendum on Carter's handling of the economy. "Are you better off now than you were four years ago?" he asked. The answer was obvious. Polls which had showed the race in a dead heat suddenly reflected a last-minute surge for Reagan. A week later Reagan won in a landslide.

Four years later Reagan fared badly in his first debate against Walter Mondale, who had shrewdly decided to throw the president off his stride with a surprise tactic. Instead of attacking Reagan as Carter had, Mondale devastatingly tossed him a compliment. "I like President Reagan," Mondale deadpanned. Reagan never recovered his equilibrium. Republicans had another explanation for Reagan's disastrous performance, the worst in his career. He'd been overprepared. Immediately following the debate, during which he appeared confused and stumbling, Nancy shouted at an aide, "What have you done to my husband?" Mondale walked away thinking "the guy is gone." Mondale added, "It's scary. He's not really up to it."

In the second debate Reagan, now under the tutelage of media wizard Roger Ailes, fared better. Asked, as he knew he would be, about his age, which had become an issue as a result of the first debate, Reagan humorously remarked, as everybody remembers, "I refuse to make my opponent's youth and inexperience an issue in this campaign." The crowd roared. So did Mondale, who smiled. Game over.

Contemporary Debates

In 1988 Dukakis appeared to have the edge over Bush going into the first of their two debates. Dukakis, after all, had been the star of his own television show, "The Advocates," in which he jousted with the country's leading lawyers and politicians. And in their first encounter he and Bush came out about even, Bush scoring points when he ridiculed Dukakis as a "card-carrying member of the ACLU [American Civil Liberties Union]," Dukakis when he returned fire: "Of course the vice president is questioning my patriotism. I don't think there's any question about that. And I resent it."

At the second debate Bush made fun of the one-liners Dukakis was using, remarking, "Is this the time to unleash our one-liners?" Then, after a dramatic pause, "That answer was as clear as Boston Harbor." But it was Dukakis's answer to the very first question of the night that defeated him. CNN's Bernard Shaw asked if Dukakis would support the death penalty if a man raped and murdered his wife. Dukakis, in robot-mode, responded with the dry answer he'd given on dozens of other occasions when reporters asked him about his opposition to capital punishment. Bush, who came across as more human, afterward referred to Dukakis as an Ice Man. The audience agreed.

In 1992 and 1996 Bill Clinton demonstrated his remarkable skills as a presidential debater, besting [Ross] Perot, [George H.W.] Bush, and [Bob] Dole. Perot in the first debate in 1992 had won more laugh lines but the second debate seemed to many to be a little too glib. When he repeated the joke he had made in the first debate, "I'm all ears," it fell flat. Bush notoriously glanced repeatedly at his watch in view of the camera. It reinforced the impression he was disdainful of the process, which the voters (rightly) took as an insult. (Free advice to all would be debaters: Pretend, even if you don't agree, that debates are vital to the survival of democracy....)

Three presidential debates have probably determined the outcome of an election: 1960 (Nixon/Kennedy), 1980 (Carter/Anderson/Reagan), and 1988 (Bush/Dukakis). All three races had one thing in common; polls showed the contests were close.... The chance that history will repeat itself—putting the victor in the debate in the White House—is palpable.

Periodical Bibliography

The following articles have been selected to supplement the diverse views presented in this chapter.

Khisu Beom, Diana B. Carlin, and Mark D. Silver — "The World Was Watching—and Talking: International Perspectives on the 2004 Presidential Debates," *American Behavioral Scientist*, October 2005.

Richard Goldstein — "Hail-to-the-Chief Show," *Nation*, February 14, 2005.

Joshua Green — "Do Polls Still Work?" *Atlantic Monthly*, November 2006.

Stefan Halper — "Big Ideas, Big Problems," *National Interest*, March/April 2007.

Michael Learmonth — "Hail to the Campaign Coin," *Variety*, January 29, 2007.

Matt Lewis — "Pack the Room: Holding a Successful Event," *Campaigns & Elections*, February 2006.

Ramesh Ponnuru — "Lies, Damned Lies, and Journalists," *National Review*, November 8, 2004.

Ira Teinowitz — "Election 2008: What's Next for Media," *Television Week*, November 13, 2006.

Elizabeth Wasserman — "Media: Small Niche, Big Impact," *CQ Weekly*, June 4, 2007.

Matt Welch — "Biased About Bias," *Reason*, December 2004.

OPPOSING VIEWPOINTS® SERIES

Chapter 4

Should the Electoral College Be Abolished or Reformed?

Chapter Preface

Few aspects of the presidential election process are as controversial as the electoral college. The institution was created by the Founding Fathers and enshrined in the Constitution. When Americans go to the polls, they do not directly elect the president. Instead, they are technically voting for a slate of electors. Each party that has a candidate on the ballot in a particular state chooses a group of electors that equals that state's congressional delegation. For instance, Arizona has two senators and eight members of the House of Representatives. Therefore the state has ten electoral votes. Prior to the election, each party picks ten people to serve as electors and if their candidate wins a majority in the polling, that candidate receives all ten electoral votes. After the election, all of the electors from each of the states meet in Washington, D.C., and formally cast their votes. There are 538 electoral votes, and to be elected president, a candidate must have a majority, or 270 electoral votes. Even if candidates receive a majority of the popular vote, if they do not win a majority of the electoral vote, they are not elected president. On four occasions in American history, a candidate has won the popular vote but lost in the electoral college. If no candidate receives a majority of the electoral votes, the House of Representatives decides the election. The last time that happened was in 1824.

The electoral college was put in place because the framers of the Constitution sought to give the states a role in electing the president. In this respect, the electoral college is an important component of the nation's federal system; however, the institution was also created as a check on the average voter. Early American political elites did not trust the judgment of ordinary Americans and saw the electoral college as a means to prevent the election of someone unsuitable for office. Consequently, some argue that the electoral college is undemocratic. Some studies also show that the institution discourages voting since some people believe that their individual vote does not matter.

The authors in the following chapter examine the electoral college in great detail. They explore the creation of the institution and its role in contemporary elections. The viewpoints also analyze various reform proposals and investigate the impact that changes in the presidential election process would have on the federal system, states, and individual voters.

Viewpoint 1

> *"Why has this anachronistic system ... survived?"*

The Electoral College Should Be Abolished

John B. Anderson

In the following viewpoint, John B. Anderson analyzes the arguments for and against the electoral college. He contends that the system was originally created as a means to enhance federalism and give the states a say in presidential elections, but that the college should now be abolished since it undermines direct democracy and the will of the people. Anderson is a former congressman and presidential candidate and is currently a law professor at Nova Southeastern University.

As you read, consider the following questions:

1. Why, according to the author, was the electoral college system included in the Constitution?
2. What were the most serious recent reform proposals for the system of presidential elections, according to Anderson?

John B. Anderson, "The Electoral College Flunks the Test in an Age of Democracy," *Human Rights* Magazine, vol. 32, issue 2, spring 2005, pp. 17–20. www.abanet.org/irr/hr.

3. According to the author, what are the main obstacles to reform of the electoral college?

The reelection of the forty-third president of the United States took place not on November 2, 2004, when some 120 million Americans cast their ballots, but on December 13, 2004, when 538 members of the Electoral College officially met pursuant to article II, section 1 of the U.S. Constitution.

This quadrennial event has not been emulated by any other democracy in the world. One American observer, Robert Pastor, director of the Center for Democracy and Election Management, who previously helped organize election observation missions to about thirty countries, recently commented that "[t]he Electoral College was a progressive innovation in the 18th Century; today, it's mainly dictatorships like Communist China that use an indirect system to choose their highest leader."

Arguments for the Electoral College

There is another interpretation of the genesis of the Electoral College that is even less kind in explaining its inclusion in the Constitution: that the Electoral College grew out of the last-ditch efforts of the "states righters" of 1787 to preserve as much of the Articles of Confederation as possible. This group was intent on denying direct popular election of the president and preserving the power of the states. Just as they succeeded in a provision allowing state legislatures to elect the members of the Senate, they wanted the primary power to elect a president to be lodged in the states—not in a mass electorate comprised of individual voters. James Madison, James Wilson, and Gouverneur Morris preferred a vote by the people but fell back on the compromise of an Electoral College to appease the die-hard defenders of the Articles of Confederation and their exaltation of each state's right to be its own principal governing force.

Bush v. Gore Reaffirmed Equal Protection Under the Law in Electoral Disputes

The courts should also stand by *Bush v. Gore*'s equal protection analysis for the simple reason that it was right (even if the remedy of stopping the recount was not). Elections that systematically make it less likely that some voters will get to cast a vote that is counted are a denial of equal protection of the law. The conservative justices may have been able to see this unfairness only when they looked at the problem from Mr. Bush's perspective, but it is just as true when the N.A.A.C.P. [National Association for the Advancement of Colored People] and groups like it raise the objection.

There is a final reason *Bush v. Gore* should survive. In deciding cases, courts should be attentive not only to the Constitution and other laws, but to whether they are acting in ways that promote an overall sense of justice. The Supreme Court's highly partisan resolution of the 2000 election was a severe blow to American democracy, and to the court's own standing. The courts could start to undo the damage by deciding that, rather than disappearing down the memory hole, *Bush v. Gore* will stand for the principle that elections need to be as fair as we can possibly make them.

Adam Cohen, New York Times, *August 15, 2006.*

The original design of the Electoral College was based on the notion that electors would be faithful agents of the people who were "men superior in discernment, virtue and information" and who acted "according to their own will." Fifty years later, Justice Joseph Bradley of the U.S. Supreme Court and a member of the 1877 Electoral Commission established to settle the disputed Hayes-Tilden Election of 1876, said, "Electors were mere instruments of party—party puppets—who are to carry out a function that an automaton without volition or intelligence might as well perform." Another commentator of the same period, Senator John J. Ingalls of Kansas, opined that "electors are like the marionettes in a Punch and Judy show."

Why has this anachronistic system, despite its demonstrable inability to survive even a test of rationality let alone fulfill the noble aspirations of the Framers, survived? Why has the U.S. Supreme Court ignored the clear evidence that the original purpose of the college has not only been subverted by faithless electors but that the whole scheme is flawed and demeans the right of individual voters to be treated equally?

In *McPherson v. Blacker*, 146 U.S. 1 (1892), relied on heavily by the Court in *Bush v. Gore*, 531 U.S. 98 (2000), the Supreme Court still insisted that the Framers expected that electors would exercise discretion in selecting a president. Even today [in 2005], in their *Bush v. Gore* concurrence, Chief Justice [William] Rehnquist and Justices [Antonin] Scalia and [Clarence] Thomas added that their inquiry did "not imply a disrespect for state courts but rather a respect for the constitutionally prescribed role of state legislatures." This obduracy in clinging to an outmoded, discredited system, whose foundation has been completely eroded by the sweeping changes in every facet of the American polity, is astonishing.

The Electoral College and Federalism

I believe that the primary reason for maintaining the Electoral College may be the argument that direct popular election would be a cancer on the federal system. One persistent, indeed ardent, defender of this archaic method of presidential selection is Judith Best, who insists direct popular election would "deform our Constitution and constitute a serious implicit attack on the federal principle."

Along with many other political observers, I have been mystified, if not confounded, by the fact that the 2000 presidential election failed to energize a strong effort to abolish the Electoral College. The voices for reform and the adoption of direct popular election have been muted. Rather, Ms. Best has been joined by Electoral College proponents like Norman Ornstein of the American Enterprise Institute, who wrote that "three (or four) crises out of more than fifty presidential elections is remarkably small." He continued: "Heaven forbid a direct vote and the 'horrific nightmare' of a possible nationwide recount in a close contest, especially with lots of late-arriving absentee votes."

At this point, one wonders if the nation's thirty-six-day wait for the announcement of the president-elect and the Supreme Court's five-to-four majority in the case was not in fact a "horrific nightmare." I believe that the occupant of the nation's highest office should be determined by legally registered voters—not 538 faceless, nameless electors—not even if their role is decreed by five members of the U.S. Supreme Court.

Reform Proposals

The most recent history of any substantial opposition to this outmoded mechanism goes back to my own days in the U.S. House of Representatives, where from 1961–1980, I represented the 16th Congressional District of Illinois. In 1969, by a vote of 338 to 10, far more than the necessary two-thirds, representatives supported a constitutional amendment that would have provided for direct election. It was, of course, defeated in the Senate, where it fell prey to a filibuster made up largely of senators from southern states, aided and abetted by conservatives from small states. The members of this camp offered arguments that were largely based on the notion that in a system of direct election they would in some way—never explained—find their own roles diminished and the needs of their states correspondingly ignored.

Another attempt a decade later failed when even liberal senators fell away from the cause on the grounds that it would be harmful to certain minority groups that they represented. At about the same time, the Twentieth Century Fund Task Force on Reform conceived a "national bonus plan." It would have added a bonus of 102 electoral votes—two for each state plus the District of Columbia—to be awarded the winner of the popular vote. Obviously, this would ensure the election of the candidate favored by the people. This idea has not won over those wedded to the concept of an Electoral College as presently constituted, however.

Other proposals have sought to move to direct election without going through the torturous amendment process. One was offered by Professors Akhil Amar and Vilram Amar, who point out that the Electoral College, as now configured, neither helps small states, ensures states' rights, nor protects the concept of federalism. Indeed, electing a president by a popular vote would provide state governments incentives to improve our democracy by finding ways to increase the size of the vote. The Amars would, it should be pointed out, favor instant runoff voting as the optimum method for conducting the direct popular vote. The rank ordering of candidates on the ballot could ensure that, with instant runoff voting, it would be possible in one and the same election to conduct the count in a manner to ensure a true majority winner. This would solve the "spoiler problem" that today confronts any candidate who chooses to run outside the present majority party duopoly.

Impediments to Reform

Our elections, as they are now held, have divided rather than united the country. Battleground states are the focus of both the candidates and the media. In the 2004 campaign, to cite only one example, President [George W.] Bush bothered to poll in only eighteen states. More importantly, most registration drives were focused on battleground states. Is it healthy for the democratic process to see the number of competitive states decreasing? Indeed, if federalism is a principal argument for some last-ditch advocates on the Electoral College in a country where an overwhelming majority of Americans favor direct election but feel increasingly ignored, it is the defenders of the status quo who should feel challenged.

Our current method of electing presidents is conducive to the twin evils of fraud and blatantly partisan election administration. Election 2004 witnessed a win by the president of approximately 119,000 votes in Ohio. Narrow margins provide an incentive for fraud and the construction of rules and regulations that promote political advantage over voters' rights.

Finally, the present system actually increases a likelihood of ties in the Electoral College. A shift of about 21,000 votes in Iowa, Nevada, and New Mexico could have thrown the election into a 269-269 electoral vote tie, which is certainly a possibility in the future as well. Once the election goes to the House of Representatives, where each state has a single vote, the likelihood of extreme partisanship and deal making, which can trump the collective will of the people that has manifested itself in the popular vote, becomes very real.

The Need for Change

The need for constitutional change is upon us, and the task is a difficult one. The dimensions of the problem are well defined in an article by Richard H. Pildes:

> [But] democratic institutional designers rarely consider or build in the capacity for representative institutions to be readily redesigned as circumstances change. The static considerations of power and vulnerability at the moment of formation overwhelm any capacity to create ready mechanisms for later institutional self-revision. To make matters

worse, one of the iron laws of democratic institutions is that institutional structures once created become refractory to change.

As specific examples in our U.S. Constitution, Pildes goes on to cite the provisions for both the Senate and the Electoral College, and the fact that the representational basis for both is skewed. In the Senate, approximately 500,000 Wyoming citizens have the same voting power as thirty-four million Californians. Pildes goes on to specifically argue that the Electoral College, with its bonus of two electoral votes for each state regardless of size, illustrates a larger design defect the Constitution's failure to include any ready capacity to modify the Electoral College structure over time through national political processes, particularly in light of the material disincentives for individual states to change their own allocation rules for electors.

Notwithstanding this more than somewhat somber assessment of the built-in resistance to constitutional change, I am encouraged by the currency of the concept of an "Age of Democracy." If we are indeed being commissioned to spread democracy around the world, we must, in Socratic fashion, know ourselves. We are compelled to look within and to strive to become the exemplar of that which we are seeking to export. Direct democracy should exist at home within the borders of the American republic. It must replace an electoral system chained to the past and its fear of giving the people themselves the ability to choose an American president.

VIEWPOINT 2

"The National Popular Vote Plan is, or should be, an embarrassment to its promoters."

Plans to Reform the Electoral College Would Harm Small States

George Detweiler

In the following viewpoint, George Detweiler defends the current electoral college system. He examines the National Popular Vote Plan, which would alter the electoral college and highlights the flaws in the proposed reforms. Among the main problems with the reform plan, he argues, are the potential for increased voter fraud and the likelihood that election by direct popular vote would decrease the political influence of small states. Detweiler is a former assistant attorney general for Idaho and a specialist in constitutional law.

As you read, consider the following questions:

1. What are the provisions of the proposed National Popular Vote Plan, as cited by Detweiler?

2. As reported by the author, can individual states choose the manner in which they select electors to the Electoral College?
3. According to Detweiler, how would the National Popular Vote Plan increase electoral fraud in presidential elections?

Assaults on the electoral college are nothing new. The left seems to keep a calendar which schedules dates for periodic attacks on the Constitution's system for electing the president and the vice president. February 23 [2006] was such a date. A press conference at the National Press Club in the nation's capital was showtime for political "has-beens" and "wannabes" from deep left field who unwrapped their latest populist project. Promoters include John B. Anderson (former independent presidential candidate), former Rep. Tom Campbell (R-Calif.), former Senators Birch Bayh (D-Ind.) and Jake Garn (R-Utah), Chellie Pingree (President, Common Cause), and others.

Rankled by any institution which they perceive as less than pure democracy, these populists proposed a National Popular Vote Plan to change the way America chooses its chief executive. Each state's legislature is encouraged to enact legislation establishing a new, uniform method of selecting presidential electors. The program involves an agreement among participating states and goes into effect when adopted by enough states to constitute a majority (270) of the votes in the electoral college. The structure of the agreement is bizarre:

- Each member state conducts a popular election for president and vice president.
- The chief election officer of each state must determine the total popular vote for president/vice president *in the entire nation* even though some states may not have subscribed to the agreement. This is denominated the "national popular vote total."

- Presidential candidates will name their own state of electors. The state election officer will appoint the state of electors pledged to the candidate who is chosen as the "national popular vote winner" to be the official electors for the state. It is now common practice for states to elect their presidential electors on the popular ballot, with the names of these electors appearing beside the presidential candidate whom they are pledged to support. This will be changed by the new system, and presidential electors will no longer be chosen by popular vote, but by one person only—the chief election officer in each member state. Note that the presidential candidate declared to be the "national popular vote winner" may thus win a state's electors even though he *lost the popular vote in that state.*
- In member states, the chief election officer's determination of the "national popular vote total" is final and no provision for recount (an impossibility since it could be a nationwide recount) is made. Neither is there provision for judicial or other relief in the event of voter fraud. Special provisions are made to break tie votes in the popular presidential vote.
- If any member state (acting only through its chief elections officer) selects too few or too many electors, the presidential candidate declared to be the "national popular vote winner" may appoint the presidential electors for that state. Note that the job of choosing the state's electors is thereby transferred to someone who is not a holder of public office nor even a citizen of the state in question.
- Any member state can withdraw from the agreement, except for a window of six months prior to the expiration of a presidential term. If the withdrawal occurs within that window, it is effective only after an intervening presidential election.

The Electoral College Is Effective

Proponents of the Electoral College claim that critics exaggerate the risks in our present system, pointing to the very small number of occasions where their concerns have come to fruition. Only two elections in our history were ever decided in the House and none since 1825. The Electoral College system also reduces the possibility of voter fraud; in a direct national election votes could be bought anywhere, even in heavily concentrated Democratic or Republican states where under the present system, few would bother to attempt such a thing. In addition, while small states may be overrepresented under the present system, under any other alternatives smaller states would virtually be ignored. Most importantly, supporters of the Electoral College would add that it is a tried and true system, one that is efficient, identifies a winner quickly, and avoids recounts. For these reasons, Americans would be foolish to risk experimenting with a new one.

Mary Frances Greene, U. S. National Archives. www.archives.gov.

- The agreement terminates automatically if the electoral college is abolished—the real goal of the plan and its supporters.

Creation of the Electoral College

The electoral college was created by Article 1, Section 1 of the Constitution, which provides: "Each State shall appoint, in such Manner as the Legislature thereof may direct, a Number of Electors, equal to the whole Number of Senators and Representatives to which the State may be entitled in Congress." The duty of the electoral college is to elect the president and the vice president in a process specified in Amendment XII. The system provides a measure of equality between the large, populous states and the smaller ones.

Does the Constitution permit a state to select its presidential electors by a means other than popular election? Yes. The electoral college's enabling provision uses the word "appoint" rather than "choose" or "elect." However, in Article 1, Section 10, the Constitution also declares: "No State shall, without the consent of Congress ... enter into any Agreement or Compact with another State." Congress would be likely to approve a National Popular Vote Plan if popular support gave the plan impetus: nevertheless, it is significant that the plan has no mention of any mechanism for securing, or even the need to get, congressional approval.

Problems with Reform Efforts

The plan is a schizophrenic nightmare. It would bind states together into an amorphous mass of voters ostensibly for popular election of presidents. Meanwhile the system reduces the less-populous states to a helpless irrelevancy. While professing "every vote equal," the system for choosing presidential electors could result in a member state selecting electors pledged to a presidential candidate who had lost the election in that state. Also, Lord Acton's adage about absolute power corrupting absolutely is exemplified in the power of the member states' chief election officer, who makes a final unappealable determination of the "national popular vote winner."

The National Popular Vote Plan becomes an invitation to corruption. Voter fraud, hard enough to prove and to remedy when done within the boundaries of any one state, becomes almost impossible to check under the plan. The National Popular Vote Plan forces one state to select electors on the basis of the popular election results for president *in other states, where there is no opportunity for the first state to contest the election*—but where significant voter fraud could have occurred.

Constitutional infirmities linger. The Constitution empowers each state legislature to determine how its presidential electors are chosen. By adopting the National Popular Vote Plan, a state delegates this power to the entire nation based on who wins the national popular vote. Both federal and state laws recognize that some powers are delegable, while others are not. Is this a power capable of delegation under either the federal or the various state constitutions? Will state or federal judges be able to grant injunctions in case of violations of election laws?

The plan is, after all, a mix of the laws of many states coupled with congressional approval. The plan itself makes no provision for such relief. In such a situation, it would be a legal stretch for a judge to grant an injunction without specific statutory authority. What happens if a state withdraws from the agreement during the six-month window and fails to wait for an intervening presidential election as required by the plan before it pursues its own election laws? No other state has jurisdiction to prevent it. The plan provides no remedy and neither does federal law. All of these issues are food for protracted, unnecessary, costly litigation.

Support for Reform

Despite the litany of infirmities, the National Popular Vote Plan has been introduced in a number of states including California. To date, none has completed the process of enacting it into law. It is important to remember that it is easier to oppose and stop bad legislation than it is to repeal it after it has passed.

The usual suspects of the left-wing press ran with the story of the National Popular Vote Plan after it was announced at the press conference. Predictably, it has the *New York Times*' endorsement. The *Times* urged state legislatures to enact it. Falling in line were the *Chicago Sun-Times*, the *Minneapolis Star Tribune*, the *Denver Post*, the *Houston Chronicle*, and others.

The National Popular Vote Plan is, or should be, an embarrassment to its promoters. To borrow a buzz word form the national education debate, it lacks "intelligent design." It is fraught with evil intentions. It must never be implemented.

VIEWPOINT 3

> *"The current system teaches us that the character of a majority is more important than its size alone."*

The Electoral College Strengthens Federalism

Michael M. Uhlmann

In the next viewpoint Michael M. Uhlmann explores the benefits of the electoral college. He argues that the system strengthens American federalism by ensuring that the states have a role to play in presidential elections and by preventing political fragmentation by perpetuating the two-party system. The electoral college also reinforces the federal system of checks and balances. Uhlmann is a professor of politics and policy at Claremont Graduate University and author of The Electoral College Book.

As you read, consider the following questions:

1. What, according to the author, would be some of the problems that would emerge if the electoral college were abolished?
2. How does the electoral college ensure limited national government and equal rights, according to Uhlmann?

Michael M. Uhlmann, "The Old (Electoral) College Cheer: Why We Have It; Why We Need It," *National Review*, vol. 56, issue 21, November 8, 2004, p. 28.

3. According to the author, how does the electoral college bolster the two-party system?

As the late Rodney Dangerfield might say, the Electoral College just don't get no respect. Polls show that most Americans, given the opportunity, would cashier it tomorrow in favor of so-called direct election. That they'd live to regret their decision only reminds us of H. L. Mencken's definition of democracy: a form of government in which the people know what they want, and deserve to get it good and hard. What the people would get by choosing direct election is the disintegration of the state-based two-party system; the rise of numerous factional parties based on region, class, ideology, or cult of personality; radicalized public opinion, frequent runoff elections, widespread electoral fraud, and centralized control of the electoral process; and, ultimately, unstable national government that veers between incompetence and tyrannical caprice. And that's only a partial list.

Dissatisfaction with the electoral-vote system has been a staple of populist rhetoric ever since presidential elections became fully democratized in the 1820s. More than 700 constitutional amendments have been introduced to change the system—by far the greatest number on any subject—and although reform prescriptions have varied greatly in detail, their common assumption has always been that our electoral rules prevent the true voice of the people from being heard.

But what is the "true voice" of the people? Public sentiment can be expressed and measured in any number of ways, but not all are conducive to securing rights. If ascertaining the consent of the people were only a matter of counting heads until you got to 50 percent plus one, we could dispense with most of the distinctive features of the Constitution—not only electoral votes, but also federalism, the separation of powers, bicameralism, and staggered elections. All of these devices depart from simple majoritarianism, and for good reason: Men do not suddenly become angels when they acquire the right to vote; an electoral majority can be just as tyrannical as autocratic kings or corrupt oligarchs.

Reasons for the Electoral College

The Founders believed that while the selfish proclivities of human nature could not be eliminated, their baleful effects could be mitigated by a properly designed constitutional structure. Although the Constitution recognizes no other source of authority than the people, it takes pains to shape and channel popular consent in very particular ways. Thomas Jefferson perfectly captured the Framers' intent in his First Inaugural Address: "All, too, will bear in mind this sacred principle, that though the will of the majority is in all cases to prevail, that will to be rightful must be reasonable; that the minority possess their equal rights, which equal law must protect, and to violate which would be oppression." By reasonable majorities, Jefferson meant those that would reflect popular sentiment but, by the very manner of their composition, would be unable or unlikely to suppress the rights and interests of those in the minority. Accordingly, the Constitution understands elections not as ends in themselves, but as a means of securing limited government and equal rights for all.

The presidential election system helps to form reasonable majorities through the interaction of its three distinguishing attributes: the distribution and apportionment of electoral votes in accordance with the federal principle; the requirement that the winner garner a majority of electoral votes; and the custom (followed by 48 of 50 states) of awarding all of a state's electoral votes to the popular-vote victor within that state. Working together, these features link the presidency to the federal system, discourage third parties, and induce moderation on the part of candidates and interest groups alike. No candidate can win without a broad national coalition, assembled state by state yet compelled to transcend narrow geographic, economic, and social interests.

The Electoral College Supports a Two-Party System

The Electoral College is part of a delicate set of constitutional checks and balances. Change one part and the whole mechanism could be thrown off. The current electoral system means that a presidential campaign has to be waged nationally by large, well-organized parties—usually two—rather than by a bunch of competing individual candidates. Or by a dozen or so small parties slugging it out to see which one can win a bare plurality.

With the Electoral College in place, the winner has got to get enough votes in enough states to claim a majority of the electors—not just a popular plurality. That means organizing large, national parties, which is how the country's two-party system came about. Take away the Electoral College, and you take away a prominent inducement for having a two-party system.

Paul Greenberg, Townhall.com, *April 4, 2007.*

Reformers tend to assume that the mode of the presidential election can be changed without affecting anything else. Not so. As Sen. John F. Kennedy argued in the 1950s, by changing the method of the presidential election, you change not only the presidency but the entire political solar system of which it is an integral part. The presidency is at once the apex of our constitutional structure and the grand prize of the party system. Our method of selecting a president is the linchpin that holds both together. Capturing the presidency is the principal raison d'être of our political parties, whose structure, thanks to the electoral-vote system, mirrors the uniquely federal structure of the Constitution. This means that two-party competition is the norm; in a country of America's size and diversity, that is no small virtue.

The Two-Party System

With (for the most part) only two parties in contention, the major candidates are forced to appeal to most of the same voters. This drives them both toward the center, moderates their campaign rhetoric, and helps the winner to govern more effectively once in office. Many factional interests, for their part, are under a reciprocal inducement to buy insurance with both sides, meaning the compromises necessary for successful rule will be made prior to and not after the election. Moreover, by making the states the principal electoral battlegrounds, the current system tends to insulate the nation against the effects of local voting fraud. All in all, the current system forces the ambitions of presidential candidates into the same constitutional mold that defines and tempers American political life as a whole. It thereby prevents the presidency from becoming a potentially dangerous tutelary force separate and apart from the rest of the Constitution's structure.

These and other salutary consequences would disappear under direct election, whose deceptive simplicities mask its truly radical character.... We came perilously close to enacting direct election following the 1968 contest, when George Wallace's third-party candidacy shattered the New Deal coalition of big-city machines and the one-party South. Fearing the long-run effects of Republican competition in the New South, Democrats tried to change the rules to their advantage. They will do so again as soon as the opportunity seems propitious....

Electoral College Reform Efforts

In 1969, as President [Richard] Nixon dithered and eventually ducked, direct election passed the House by a sizeable constitutional majority—including many Republicans who ought to have known better. But for a small and determined group of conservative Democratic and Republican senators who filibustered it to death, direct election would have been presented to the states in an atmosphere that greatly favored ratification. Sensible heads may prevail in today's ... House, but don't count on it: On matters of electoral reform especially, congressmen have little stomach for resisting populist enthusiasms. A House that rolled over for McCain-Feingold [a campaign financing bill], which enjoyed only mild public support, will not likely oppose the clamor for direct election. As for today's Senate, one would be hard pressed to identify a band of constitutional stalwarts comparable to those who courageously resisted popular currents in 1970. The next few years, in short, may test whether our nation has the patience or wisdom to preserve the delicate balances of our constitutional solar system.

The Electoral College and Federalism

Proponents of direct election indict those delicate balances for being "undemocratic." That is true only in the most superficial sense. If the Electoral College is undemocratic, so are federalism, the United States Senate, and the procedure for constitutional amendment. So is bicameralism and, for that matter, the separation of powers, which among other things authorizes an unelected judiciary. These constitutional devices were once widely understood to be the very heart and soul of the effort to form reasonable majorities. If all you care about is the achievement of mathematical equality in presidential elections, and if to achieve that goal you're willing to eliminate the states' role in presidential elections, what other "undemocratic" features of the Constitution are you also willing to destroy? And when you're done hacking your way through the Constitution, what guarantee can you give that your mathematically equal majorities can be restrained? How will you constrain the ambitions of presidents who claim to be the only authentic voice of the people?

The current system teaches us that the character of a majority is more important than its size alone. Americans ought to care about whether the winner's support is spread across a broad geographic area and a wide spectrum of interests. That is what enables presidents to govern more effectively—and what encourages them to govern more justly than they would if their majority were gathered from, say, an aggregation of heavy population centers. By ensuring that the winner's majority reflects the diversity of our uniquely federated republic, the current system also assures his opposition that it will not have to fear for its life, liberty, or property. Direct election can provide no such assurance and may, in fact, guarantee just the opposite.

VIEWPOINT 4

> *"There have been about 700 failed proposals in Congress to change the electoral college system."*

The Electoral College Weakens Federalism

Randy Dotinga

In the following viewpoint, Randy Dotinga asserts that the electoral college undermines federalism since it forces candidates to spend most of their time in a few key states, thereby ignoring most of the rest of the country. The author also argues that the system leaves open the possibility that someone could become president without a majority of the vote, and it only allows for those presidential hopefuls that can appeal to broad groups of voters. Dotinga is a reporter for the Christian Science Monitor.

As you read, consider the following questions:

1. What would the National Popular Vote plan require states to do with their electoral votes, according to Dotinga?
2. According to the author, what has to happen before the National Popular Vote plan would take effect?

Randy Dotinga, "A Backdoor Plan to Thwart the Electoral College," *Christian Science Monitor*, vol. 98, issue 141, June 16, 2006, pp. 1, 10. www.csmonitor.com.

3. How, according to Dotinga, does the current system force presidential candidates to appeal to the majority of Americans?

Picture it: On election day in some future year, a presidential candidate ends up with the most popular votes but not enough electoral votes to win.

It's a repeat of the 2000 election in which one contender, Democrat Al Gore, took the majority of the national popular vote, while the other, Republican George W. Bush, clinched the most electoral college votes and, hence, the presidency.

But this time there's a twist: A bunch of states team up and give all their electoral college votes to the nationwide popular-vote winner, regardless of who won the most votes in their state. Then, the candidate who garners the most citizen votes in the country moves into the White House.

Legislative houses in Colorado and California have approved this plan, known as the National Popular Vote proposal, taking it partway to passage. Other states, too, are exploring the idea of a binding compact among states that would oblige each of them to throw its electoral votes behind the national popular-vote winner.

At issue is the nation's presidential election system governed by the electoral college. Established by the US Constitution in 1787, the system has occasionally awarded the presidency to candidates who couldn't muster the most votes nationwide, as happened in 1824, 1876, 1888, and 2000.

While an amendment to the Constitution could change or eliminate the electoral college, battleground states and small states would probably oppose any change that would leave them with less influence. Indeed, since the system's inception, numerous efforts to amend it have been defeated.

Instead, reformers have turned to the interstate compact, saying it would be constitutional because agreements between states already exist.

Advantages of Reform

The compact is designed to take effect only if states representing 270 electoral votes approve the compact legislation, giving those states majority control of the electoral college. The result: The "compact" group of states would be able to determine a presidential election.

The plan is supported by electoral reform activists and a bipartisan advisory group including former GOP [Republican] Rep. John Anderson (a presidential candidate in 1980) and former Sen. Birch Bayh (D).

They say the compact would allow long-ignored states to get attention again in presidential campaigns. The current system has "just taken a lot of states off of the presidential map," complains Rob Richie, executive director of FairVote, a nonpartisan organization based in Maryland, which supports the compact.

The compact proposal passed the California Assembly on May 30 [2006] with all but one Republican opposing. It awaits a vote in the state Senate and, if it passes, approval or rejection by Gov. Arnold Schwarzenegger (R), who hasn't publicly expressed an opinion about it.

Colorado's Senate approved the plan in April [2006] with bipartisan support, but it has not [yet] advanced....

Five GOP Assembly members are pushing a popular-vote bill in New York, and legislators in Missouri, Louisiana, and Illinois have introduced bills. Advocates hope to put the legislation before every state by 2007, says Mr. Ritchie.

Meanwhile, several newspapers have come out in favor of the plan, including *The New York Times*, which calls it an "ingenious solution."

Criticisms of Reform Plans

But in California, GOP Assemblyman Chuck DeVore derisively refers to the proposal as a way to "amend the Constitution without amending the Constitution."

Electoral College Reform Would Nationalize Campaigns

Candidates would be compelled to spread their message nationwide, instead of focusing their time and money on the battleground states. In the 2004 race, the campaigns spent 99 percent of their money and 92 percent of their time in 16 states, according to National Popular Vote figures.

"We deserve to have a national discussion when electing the president, not a discussion in five or 10 states," said Vermont state Rep. Chris Pearson of the Progressive Party.

But the proposal's foes argue that it would steer the presidential campaigns toward the more populous states and away from the smaller, rural states. In the Colorado floor debate, state Sen. Shawn Mitchell argued that the bill would make the state's voters "irrelevant."

Valerie Richardson, Washington Times, *January 31, 2007.*

"It's like cheating," says Mr. DeVore, who predicts that the plan would force candidates to campaign primarily in urban areas with large populations to win the popular vote.

Under the current system "we discourage regional candidacies and basically force people who are running for president to have a message that resonates with the vast middle of America," he says.

DeVore supports a system that would allocate some of a state's electoral votes based on the popular vote in congressional districts, an approach that exists in Nebraska and Maine. All other states and the District of Columbia award all their electoral votes to the presidential candidate who gets the most votes in their state.

It takes 270 electoral votes out of 538 total votes in the college to win the presidency. That total equals the number of members each state has in both houses of Congress, with the District of Columbia getting three of its own.

The electoral college system is "distinctly American," says Shaun Bowler, a political scientist at the University of California, Riverside.

A Controversial System

In US history, there have been about 700 failed proposals in Congress to change the electoral college system, according to the Office of the Federal Register.

"It's safe to say that there has been no aspect of what the founders worked up in Philadelphia that has received more criticism than the electoral college," says historian Rick Shenkman of George Mason University.

If any state approves this new proposal, legal challenges are inevitable, Bowler says.

But he figures there might be a way to dampen enthusiasm. "You could say the French elect their president directly," he says. "I'm thinking that will get people running away from any support: If the French do it, is it really right for the US?"

Periodical Bibliography

The following articles have been selected to supplement the diverse views presented in this chapter.

Anthony J. Bennett	"The Electoral College," *Politics Review*, September 2006.
Robert W. Bennett	"Taming the Electoral College," *Harvard Law Review*, December 2006.
Barbara Boxer	"The Count Every Vote Act of 2005," *Human Rights*, Spring 2005.
Ross Douthat, Marshall Poe, and Terrence Henry	"The Purpling of America," *Atlantic Monthly*, November 2005.
David Hill and Seth C. McKee	"The Electoral College, Mobilization, and Turnout in the 2000 Presidential Election," *American Politics Research*, September 2005.
Alexander Keyssar	"The Electoral College Flunks," *New York Times Review of Books*, March 24, 2005.
Thomas Mann	"Redistricting Reform," *National Voter*, June 2005.
Robert Richie	"Reforming the Electoral College with Interstate Compacts," *National Civic Review*, Spring 2007.
Rachel Saffron	"Electoral College Math," *Campaigns & Elections*, April 2005.

For Further Discussion

Chapter 1

1. Stephen J. Wayne traces the rise of the modern presidential election process and points out many of the benefits of current practices, while Larry J. Sabato is highly critical of the current system. What are the main areas of disagreement between the two authors? Are there any points on which the two agree? If so, what are they?
2. Based on the viewpoints in the chapter, how important are the national conventions in the nomination process? According to Jonathan Mott and Shad Satterthwaite, what are the main purposes of the modern convention?
3. Cullen Murphy is very critical of the role played by states such as New Hampshire and Iowa in the presidential election cycle. Do you agree with his choice for the most representative state? Which state in your opinion might provide a better cross-section of the United States? Why?

Chapter 2

1. Joseph E. Cantor writes about the number of ways in which the United States is unique in how it finances its elections. Cantor contends that these distinctive practices reflect the characteristics of American politics and culture. Is his argument persuasive? Why or why not? What are the main weaknesses in his argument?
2. John Samples works at the libertarian Cato Institute, an organization that generally favors limited government and a reduced federal role in American society. Does the author's place of employment influence the way you view his viewpoint? Why or why not?

3. Newt Gingrich was formerly the Speaker of the House of Representatives and a leader in the Republican Party. Does that make him a more credible author on the topic than scholars or other researchers who have never held elected office? Why or why not?

Chapter 3

1. Pam Frost Gorder contends that media coverage is generally fair, while John O'Sullivan asserts that the press is often biased against conservative candidates. What are the main differences in the arguments of the two authors?
2. Stephen F. Hayes highlights several case studies of media bias in American politics. Why does Hayes believe that the press favored John Kerry over George W. Bush in the 2004 presidential election? Are his arguments persuasive? Explain your answer.
3. How important do you believe presidential debates are to the election process? What are the main examples that Richard Shenkman cites to prove that these events can influence the outcomes of presidential elections?

Chapter 4

1. John B. Anderson argues that the original reasons behind the creation of the electoral college do not apply in today's world. Are his arguments convincing? Why or why not?
2. Several authors in the chapter use federalism as a reason to either support the electoral college or oppose it. Which author does the best job of linking federalism to the continuation of the electoral college, and why?

Organizations to Contact

The editors have compiled the following list of organizations concerned with the issues debated in this book. The descriptions are derived from materials provided by the organizations. All have publications or information available for interested readers. The list was compiled on the date of publication of the present volume; the information provided here may change. Be aware that many organizations take several weeks or longer to respond to inquiries, so allow as much time as possible.

American National Election Studies (ANES)
PO Box 1248, Ann Arbor, MI 48106-1248
(734) 764-5494 • fax: (734) 764-3341
e-mail: anes@electionstudies.org
Web site: www.electionstudies.org

The American National Election Studies is a collaborative project of the Center for Political Studies at the University of Michigan and Stanford University that is funded by the National Science Foundation. ANES analyzes why Americans vote the way they do. ANES conducts pre- and post-election studies of voters. These data are made available to politicians, the media, and teachers for use in educating the public about the importance of issues.

Campaign Finance Institute (CFI)
1990 M St. NW, Suite 380, Washington, DC 20036
(202) 969-8890 • fax: (202) 969 5612
e-mail: info@cfinst.org
Web site: www.cfinst.org

The Campaign Finance Institute is a nonprofit and nonpartisan research organization that studies issues related to campaign finance and develops reports and recommendations for government officials and the general public. CFI tracks contributions and spending by individual candidates for the presidency and Congress, as well as the fund-raising of the political parties. The majority of CFI's publications are free and available for download from their Web site.

Campaign Legal Center (CLC)
1640 Rhode Island Ave. NW, Suite 650
Washington, DC 20036
(202) 736-2200 • fax: (202) 736-2222
e-mail: info@campaignlegalcenter.org
Web site: www.campaignlegalcenter.org

The Campaign Legal Center is a nonprofit research and public advocacy organization that examines campaign finance issues and media laws related to elections and fund-raising. The CLC tracks legal cases on campaign finance and issues reports and comments to the Federal Election Commission. The CLC's Media Policy Program lobbies on behalf of open broadcast airwaves and participates in public forums on campaign media legislation. The organization also monitors actions by the Internal Revenue Service related to campaign financing.

Cato Institute
1000 Massachusetts Ave. NW, Washington, DC 20001
(202) 842-0200 • fax: (202) 842-3490
e-mail: pr@cato.org
Web site: www.cato.org

The Cato Institute was founded in 1977 by Edward H. Crane. It is a nonprofit, libertarian public-policy research center that promotes limited government, free enterprise, and individual choice. Its major research areas include budget and tax policy, constitutional studies, defense and national security, government and politics, and libertarian philosophy. The institute holds regular seminars and symposiums on public policy, and it sponsors a variety of publications, many of which are available for free through the Cato Web site.

Center for Competitive Politics (CCP)
901 N. Glebe Rd., Suite 900, Arlington, VA 22203

(703) 682-9359 • fax: (703) 682-9321
e-mail: info@campaignfreedom.org
Web site: www.campaignfreedom.org

The Center for Competitive Politics was founded as a nonprofit organization in 2005 by former Federal Elections Commission chairman Bradley A. Smith. The CCP publishes legal briefs on campaign finance, as well as prepares reports and studies on the issue. The CCP seeks to promote a more fair and open electoral process. Members of the center often testify before Congress and other public bodies, and transcripts of their presentations, as well as other documents, can be found on the CCP Web site.

Common Cause
1133 Nineteenth St. NW, 9th Floor, Washington, DC 20036
(202) 833-1200
Web site: www.commoncause.org

Common Cause is a nonprofit, nonpartisan advocacy group founded in 1970 to hold elected leaders accountable to the American people. Common Cause is active in campaign reform efforts, including campaign finance reform and stronger ethics regulations. Common Cause has led voter mobilization drives prior to presidential elections and has led efforts to enact public financing of elections at the state level. The organization has chapters in thirty-six states. Its Web site has an archive of its online journal, *Common Cause Magazine.*

Democratic National Committee (DNC)
430 South Capitol St. SE, Washington, DC 20003
(202) 863-8000
Web site: www.democrats.org

The Democratic National Committee is the governing body of the Democratic Party in the United States. The organization provides information on major national and state issues. It also offers details on how to get involved in political campaigns. The DNC is highly critical of Republican presidential candidates but provides information on Democratic candidates and campaign events. The DNC Web site examines contemporary legislation and legal issues from a Democratic perspective, as well as providing details about the party organization and structure.

Federal Elections Commission (FEC)
999 E St. NW, Washington, DC 20463
(800) 424-9530
Web site: www.fec.gov

The Federal Elections Commission oversees presidential elections in the United States and regulates campaign finance for all federal balloting, including enforcement of electoral law. The FEC's Web site contains a wealth of information about presidential elections. The FEC tracks contributions to individual candidates and political parties, including the average size of each contribution. It also provides details about the major groups and organizations that donate to campaigns. The commission's Web site has links to historical data on presidential and other federal elections.

Green Party of the United States
1700 Connecticut Ave. NW, Suite 404
Washington, DC 20009
(202) 319-7191 • fax: (202) 319-7193
e-mail: office@gp.org
Web site: www.gp.org

The Green Party was re-formed in the United States in 2001 as a national body for a number of existing state organizations. In 2000, Ralph Nader was the Green Party candidate, and in 2004 it was David Cobb. The Greens emphasize responsible environmental policies and sustainable economic development. The Green Party's Web site provides information on the party's platforms and presidential nomination process, including state primaries.

League of Women Voters
1730 M St. NW, Suite 1000, Washington, DC 20036-4508
(202) 429-1965 • fax: (202) 429-0854
Web site: www.lwv.org

Founded in 1920, the nonpartisan League of Women Voters has campaigned for a variety of causes in its history through voter education and advocacy on behalf of open elections and campaigns. Originally founded to promote voting and political participation by women, the league previously sponsored presidential debates and currently supports campaign finance reform. In addition to the national organization, there are nine hundred state and local chapters divided among the fifty states and Puerto Rico.

National Association of Secretaries of State (NASS)
444 North Capitol St. NW, Suite 401, Washington, DC 20001
(202) 624-3525 • fax: (202) 624-3527
e-mail: info@nass.org
Web site: www.nass.org

The National Association of Secretaries of State is the nonpartisan organization of the top election officials of each of the fifty states. NASS provides citizens with a range of information about elections and voting. It also advocates on behalf of election officials. NASS was one of the first bodies to oppose early primaries and caucuses; instead, it supports a rotating system that would allow different states to hold the opening primaries and would divide the country into four regions.

Project Vote Smart
One Common Ground, Philipsburg, MT 59858
(888) 868-3762
e-mail: comments@vote-smart.org
Web site: www.vote-smart.org

Project Vote Smart is a nonprofit, nonpartisan organization, that promotes voter participation and education in the United States. The organization uses volunteers and student interns to conduct a National Political Awareness Test (NPAT) prior to each election. The NPAT provides a means to learn candidates' positions on various national issues and serves as a voting guide and informational tool for the press. The project also maintains biographical information on candidates and comparisons of officials' voting records and their public stances on issues.

Reform Party
PO Box 3236, Abilene, TX 79604
(325) 672-2575
e-mail: info@reformparty.org
Web site: www.reformparty.org

The Reform Party was founded in 1995 by Ross Perot, who ran for the presidency as an independent in 1992, and again in 1996. (The party's 2000 candidate was Pat Buchanan.) This populist party emphasizes responsible government, term limits, and a balanced federal budget. The party's Web site contains its platform and principles as well as links to state organizations, overviews of candidates, and other political organizations.

Republican National Committee (RNC)
310 First St. SE, Washington, DC 20003
(202) 863-8500
Web site: www.gop.com

The Republican National Committee is the governing body of the Grand Old Party, or Republican Party. This political group offers people details on significant national and state issues, as well as information on political involvement and voter guides. The RNC is very critical of Democratic presidential candidates; however, it presents a lot of information on Republican candidates, primaries, and campaign events. The RNC Web site analyzes issues from a Republican perspective and provides an overview of the party's organization and structure.

Bibliography

Books

Bruce Ackerman and Ian Ayres	*Voting with Dollars*. New Haven, CT: Yale University Press, 2004.
Michael Barone and Richard E. Cohen	*The Almanac of American Politics, 2006*. Washington, DC: National Journal Group, 2005.
Robert W. Bennett	*Taming the Electoral College*. Stanford, CA: Stanford University Press, 2006.
Bruce Bimber and Richard Davis	*Campaigning Online: The Internet in U.S. Elections*. New York: Oxford University Press, 2003.
Jeffrey Birnbaum	*The Money Men: The Real Story of Fund-Raising's Influence on Political Power in America*. New York: Crown, 2000.
Paul Boller	*Presidential Candidates: From George Washington to George W. Bush*. New York: Oxford University Press, 2004.
Bruce Buchanan	*The Policy Partnership: Presidential Elections and American Democracy*. New York: Routledge, 2004.
James W. Caesar and Andrew E. Busch	*Red over Blue: The 2004 Elections and American Politics*. Lanham, MD: Rowman & Littlefield, 2005.

Susan J. Carroll and Richard Logan Fox, eds. *Gender and Elections: Shaping the Future of American Politics*. New York: Cambridge University Press, 2006.

Ann N. Crigler, Marion R. Just, and Edward J. McCaffery, eds. *Rethinking the Vote: The Politics and Prospects of American Electoral Reform*. New York: Oxford University Press, 2002.

William Crotty *A Defining Moment: The Presidential Election of 2004*. New York: M.E. Sharpe, 2005.

E.D. Dover *Images, Issues, and Attacks: Television Advertising by Incumbents and Challengers in Presidential Elections*. Lanham, MD: Lexington Books, 2006.

George C. Edwards III *Why the Electoral College Is Bad for America*. New Haven, CT: Yale University Press, 2004.

George Farah *No Debate: How the Republican and Democratic Parties Secretly Control the Presidential Debates*. New York: Seven Stories, 2004.

Stephen J. Farnsworth and S. Robert Lichter *The Nightly News Nightmare: Television's Coverage of U.S. Presidential Elections, 1988–2004*. Lanham, MD: Rowman & Littlefield, 2007.

Mark Green *Selling Out: How Big Corporate Money Buys Elections, Rams Through Legislation, and Betrays Our Democracy*. New York: HarperCollins, 2002.

Mark Halperin and John F. Harris	*The Way to Win: Taking Back the White House in 2008*. New York: Random House, 2006.
David Hopkins	*Presidential Elections: Strategies and Structures of American Politics*. Lanham, MD: Rowman & Littlefield, 2007.
Kevin T. Jones	*The Role of Televised Debates in the U.S. Presidential Election Process (1960–2000)*. New Orleans: University Press of the South, 2005.
Lynda Lee Kaid et al., eds.	*The Millennium Election: Communication in the 2000 Election*. Lanham, MD: Rowman & Littlefield, 2003.
Chris Katsaropoulos	*Every Vote Counts: A Practical Guide to Choosing the Next President*. Indianapolis: Que, 2005.
Jim A. Kuypers	*Press Bias and Politics: How the Media Frame Controversial Issues*. Westport, CT: Praeger, 2002.
Michael J. Malbin	*The Election After Reform: Money, Politics, and the Bipartisan Campaign Reform Act*. Lanham, MD: Rowman & Littlefield, 2006.
Nelson W. Polsby and Aaron Wildavsky	*Presidential Elections: Strategies and Structures of Americans Politics*. Lanham, MD: Rowman & Littlefield, 2004.

Larry Sabato — *Divided States of America: The Slash and Burn Politics of the 2004 Presidential Election*. New York: Longman, 2005.

John Samples — *The Fallacy of Campaign Finance Reform*. Chicago: University of Chicago Press, 2006.

Arthur Sanders — *Losing Control: Presidential Elections and the Decline of Democracy*. New York: Peter Lang, 2007.

Alan Schroeder — *Presidential Debates: Forty Years of High-Risk TV*. New York: Columbia University Press, 2000.

Paul D. Schumaker and Burdett A. Loomis, eds. — *Choosing a President: The Electoral College and Beyond*. New York: Chatham House, 2002.

Diana K. Sergis — *Bush v. Gore: Controversial Presidential Election Case*. Berkeley Heights, NJ: Enslow, 2003.

D.R. Shaw — *The Race to 270: The Electoral College and the Campaign Strategies of 2000 and 2004*. Chicago: University of Chicago Press, 2006.

Robert Shogan — *Bad News: Where the Press Goes Wrong in the Making of the President*. Chicago: Ivan R. Dee, 2001.

William David Sloan and Jenn Burleson — *Media Bias: Finding It, Fixing It*. Jefferson, NC: McFarland, 2007.

Bradley Smith	*Unfair Speech: The Folly of Campaign Finance Reform*. Princeton, NJ: Princeton University Press, 2001.
James A. Thurber and Candice J. Nelson, eds.	*Campaigns and Elections American Style*. Boulder, CO: Westview, 2004.
Robert P. Watson	*Counting Votes: Lessons from the 2000 Election in Florida*. Gainesville: University Press of Florida, 2004.
Robert P. Watson and Ann Gordon, eds.	*Anticipating Madam President*. Boulder, CO: Lynne Rienner, 2003.

Index

O

P

W

X